THE

CHRONICLES

TRACING THE HOLY GRAIL
FROM THE LAST SUPPER
TO ITS CURRENT LOCATION

E.C. COLEMAN

Doubt not,
go forward;
if thou doubt,
the beasts
will tear thee piecemeal.

The Holy Grail.
Alfred, Lord Tennyson

First published 2010

The History Press
The Mill, Brimscombe Port
Stroud, Gloucestershire, GL5 2QG
www.thehistorypress.co.uk

British Library Cataloguing in Publication Data.
A catalogue record for this book is available from the British Library.

ISBN 978 0 7524 5532 7

Typesetting and origination by The History Press
Printed in Great Britain
Manufacturing managed by Jellyfish Print Solutions Ltd

THE

Grail

CHRONICLES

CONTENTS

Introduction   7

1   The Discovery of the Lance   11
2   Queen Eleanor and the Grail   18
3   The Angevin Ascent   25
4   The Becket Challenge   30
5   The Templar Response   38
6   The Arthurian Dawn   63
7   The Lionheart Crusade   80
8   The Murder of King John   97
9   William Marshal – Guardian of the Grail   112
10   The Holy Blood and the Dominicans   120
11   The Final Guardian   134

Epilogue   155
Selected Bibliography   160
Index   163

INTRODUCTION

In 1889 a group of workmen, charged with the repair of the floor of the Angel Choir in the great church, were faced with the task of raising a large slab of mottled blue-black Portland marble. Using stout sheer legs and substantial pulleys, they managed to prise the slab from the floor and put it to one side. Clearing away less than 2ft of sand and rubble, they came across blocks of limestone. Beneath these was found a stone tomb-chest, which they knew to be the final resting place of a thirteenth-century bishop. The chest was 7ft 3in long and 2ft 8in wide. When the lid was raised, the workmen saw that the body was encased in sheets of soldered lead beneath a continuous sheet of the same metal, supported by iron bars, which covered the top. With the lead removed, the onlookers were faced with an almost complete skeleton of a man. Bizarrely, the whole of the skull was missing, with no trace of bone or teeth remaining. Although the skull had vanished, there remained a substantial amount of red-brown hair on a lead-encased block of oak that had once supported a cushion. What was left of the skeleton was dressed in the decaying vestments of a bishop and, on the left side of the bones, lay a crumbling wooden crosier, its crook carved with ornamental leaves. Between the leg bones, a massive gold finger ring holding a large rock crystal lay where it had fallen from the decaying fingers of the grave's occupant.

To the left of the skeleton, covered by a length of linen, the archaeologists found a chalice and a paten with the cup still standing upright, as it had been placed almost 600 years earlier. The paten, with a diameter of 4¾in and made of silver, bore upon it an incised representation of a hand with two fingers raised together in the form of a blessing.

The entirely undecorated chalice was also made of silver, but it had at some time been gilded. Much of the gilt overlay remained on the inside of the shallow bowl. With a height of 4½in, and with both the bowl and the disc-like foot having a 4in diameter, the chalice was completed by a stem linking the bowl and foot. Halfway up the stem, a knop – a circular protuberance – aided the user in maintaining a secure grip upon the vessel. Although completely without decoration, the chalice had a simple elegance rendered slightly homely by the use of plainly visible rivets to join the different parts of the stem.

Finding such artefacts in the tomb of a bishop was not at all unusual. Similar items had been found in the tombs of two previous bishops and this may well have been normal practice in the Middle Ages. But this chalice was different – this chalice might be the stuff of heroic legend and quest. This chalice could be the Holy Grail.

But why should this particular chalice be the most revered and mysterious lost item in the western world? Especially as it does not appear amongst the earliest and most holy relics of Christ, which were the True Cross, the Crown of Thorns, the Nails used in Christ's Crucifixion and the Lance (or Spear) used to wound Christ in the side as he hung upon the Cross. The Holy Grail, on the other hand, appeared only in the latter decades of the thirteenth century. It then became firmly embedded in obscure, and almost forgotten, tales surrounding a mythical king, only to resurface at the hands of Victorian poets and artists.

How do we know that the Holy Grail was even a chalice? In its first appearance in literature, the Grail was more likely to have been a dish, and not even a very important one at that. The writer referred to '*a* graal' which bore a sacramental host or wafer. This use of the word 'graal' suggests an origin in the Latin word '*gradalis*', meaning simply a dish or platter. Shortly afterwards, the dish became a chalice known as '*the* Graal'. It did not, however, stay solely in that form. It also appeared as a sacred stone, as a closely guarded secret, as Christ's still-existing bloodline or as two stones brought to England by Admiral Lord George Anson.

Even as a chalice, the Holy Grail appears to have arisen from two, or perhaps three, sources. Firstly, it was supposed to be the cup used by Christ at the Last Supper. Or, on the other hand, it was the cup used to catch the blood of Christ as his corpse was pierced by the Lance. Further still, it could have been a single cup used at both events.

The cup used by Christ at the Last Supper is mentioned in the Gospels by Saints Mark and Luke. It is also mentioned by Paul in his Letters to the Corinthians. In the Authorised Version of the New Testament, only St John mentions the Lance ('one of the soldiers with a spear pierced his side'), but does not reveal the soldier's name. William Wake, Archbishop of Canterbury between 1716 and 1737, does, conversely, give the name in his translation of the 'Forbidden Gospels'. In this work, Chapter VII, verse 8, of the Gospel of Nicodemus, reads: 'Then Longinus, a certain soldier, taking a spear, pierced his side, and presently there came forth blood and water.' Nowhere, however, is there mention of a cup used to collect the blood from Christ's wound.

It appears, nevertheless, that a cup, of one form or another, played a part in the last days of Christ's time on Earth, either as a simple domestic implement (an almost incontrovertible fact) or, as far as practising Christians are concerned, as one of the vital elements of the Eucharist or Holy Communion. What shape that cup was, from what it was made, whether it was plain or decorated, remains unknown.

How then could an artefact, about which almost nothing is known, take on the definitive shape of a chalice, become the objective of mythical quest and end up in the tomb of an English bishop?

E.C. Coleman

1

THE DISCOVERY
OF THE LANCE

It would be quite unthinkable for the followers of someone such as Christ to depart without obtaining something with which to mark their time in His presence. Whether it was just a handful of sand on which He had walked or the empty shroud from His tomb, His followers, disciples and even the Apostles would have held on to whatever they could as precious mementoes of their hope and inspiration. On the substance of such items are relics created, which the faithful revere as creating an invisible thread of fidelity to God and to His Son.

Sadly, with human nature being fashioned as it is, the existence of relics, whether from Christ Himself or from the cavalcade of saints that followed Him, tended to become more prolific as they became equally more fraudulent. However, to the followers of Christ, it was belief in the relic that mattered. It was belief that created the invisible thread, and if awestruck peasants gazed upon one of hundreds of thorns from the Crown of Thorns, couched in a casket that was more valuable than their entire lifetimes' income, it was enough for them to believe. They would not question its authenticity, but trust in the clergy placed over them by God's command.

The Angel Choir of Lincoln Cathedral in 1819. The female figure is standing at the foot of the tomb opened in 1889. The column rising up immediately above the visitors divides to form the arches. At the point of division can be found the Lincoln Imp. To the right of the base of the same column can be seen the remains of the Head Shrine of St Hugh.

When the Apostle Peter travelled north to Antioch after Christ's Crucifixion, it is more than probable that he would be carrying such relics. Peter, probably closer to Christ than any of the other Apostles, would not have left without mementoes of his time with the Saviour. Furthermore, being so close to the centre of events, Peter would have had greater access to what was available and may have had in his possession the tip of the Lance and the cup which legend later claimed to be the vessel that was used to collect the blood of Christ. Whatever he may have had, if anything, they helped to make Antioch the first centre of the worship of Christ and the place where the word 'Christian' was born.

The rise of Islam in the early seventh century saw a bloody swathe of conflict which, in less than a century, saw the followers of Muhammad reach as far east as the Punjab and as far west as the Atlantic Ocean. In AD 711 they invaded Europe through the Iberian Peninsular and, by AD 732, had reached as far north as Poitiers. There, just north of the city, the Muslim invaders were defeated by the Frankish leader Charles Martel, who drove them back south of the Pyrenees.

Over a thousand years after the arrival of St Peter in Antioch, the Holy Land of the Christians had become a seething cauldron of Islamic conflict. Whole nations, tribes and sects fell upon each other in the name of the Prophet as the Seljuk Turks, taking advantage of the chaos, pushed as far west as the shores of the Black Sea, the Bosphorus, the Aegean Sea and the Mediterranean. They also advanced to the south along the eastern Mediterranean coasts, where they clashed with Fatimid Arabs who, earlier, had expanded out of Egypt as far north as Syria.

A silver plaque found in Antioch showing St Peter. A chalice is placed just beneath his feet while a spearhead he is holding develops into a Cross.

In 1009 the Fatimids had shocked Christianity by destroying Jerusalem's Church of the Holy Sepulchre, built by St Helen, the mother of the Emperor Constantine. Only after accepting a huge bribe from the Constantinople-based Eastern Orthodox Byzantine Empire, did the Fatimids permit the rebuilding of the church and allow pilgrims to visit the site. But it was an uneasy truce and, in the following years, many pilgrims and clergy were attacked and killed.

Despite the Great Schism of 1054, which had divided the Christian Church into the Latin Roman Catholic Church and the Eastern Orthodox Church, the Byzantine Emperor Alexios I appealed to Pope Urban II for help against the Muslims now amassing within sight of Constantinople. With the approval of the Pope, the first response to the request came from Peter the Hermit, a charismatic preacher who, setting out from Cologne in 1095 with thousands of mainly unarmed followers, reached the city the following year. Alexios, unimpressed by this ragged band, sent them across the Bosphorus where the majority were slaughtered or taken as slaves by the Turks.

The next arrivals at Constantinople were of a very different stamp. Under the leadership of Godfrey of Bouillon, Raymond IV of Toulouse and Bohemund of Taranto, thousands of heavily armed and well-trained soldiers crossed over to Asia Minor. All had 'taken up the Cross' in a promise to recapture Jerusalem from the Muslims. In exchange, the Pope granted them indulgences, which cleared them of the guilt of past sins and guaranteed them a swift passage to Heaven if they lost their lives in the great cause. The lands and properties of the leaders were protected from neighbouring lords in their absence and their families were guaranteed the right of succession if they lost their lives.

Victory against the Muslims was not long in coming. The city of Nicaea fell in June 1097 (although the western Crusaders were tricked by Alexios who entered the city first, thus robbing the Crusaders of their chance to plunder) and most of western Asia Minor was recaptured at the Battle of Dorylaion in the following month. Soon the Crusaders arrived at Antioch and laid siege to the city, which had been captured by the Turks in 1085. Fending off attacks from supporting Muslim armies and the city itself, the Crusaders were surprised to see the approach of a Fatimid delegation who offered to let them have the whole of Syria without molestation if they promised not to attack Fatimid territories to the south. However, as these territories included Jerusalem, the Crusaders declined the offer.

As the siege dragged on, the Byzantine ambassador to the Crusade decided to leave. This apparent desertion led to the Crusader leaders abandoning a previous promise made to Alexios to hand all territorial gains over to the Byzantine Empire. Instead, they would keep all gains for themselves.

In the first days of June 1098, Antioch was taken after a traitor was bribed to open the gates. After the routine massacre of the defenders, Bohemund declared himself Prince of Antioch and settled down to defend the city from a Muslim army that had surrounded it only days later.

A few days into the siege, Raymond of Toulouse was approached by a monk named Peter Bartholomew who told him that he had had a number of visions. In these visions, St Andrew had taken the monk to St Peter's Cathedral in Antioch and pointed out the spot where the Lance used to pierce Christ's side was buried. Sceptical but intrigued, Raymond took Peter and a few other monks to the church and began to excavate. After a reasonably large hole had been dug, Raymond was on the point of giving up when Peter jumped into the hole, reached down and pulled out the iron tip of a spear. Another monk, who was well respected and whose word could be trusted, declared that he had seen the tip in the ground just before Peter extracted it from the soil.

Not everyone was convinced, however. Bohemund always refused to accept that the object was genuine and frequently mocked those who believed in it. Even more importantly, the papal legate to the Crusaders, Adhemar de Monteil (known as Adhemar de la Puy from his appointment as Bishop of Puy-en-Velay), also refused to accept the so-called relic. He had seen the genuine Lance in Constantinople where it had ended up after being seen on several occasions in the Church of the Holy Sepulchre at Jerusalem. On the other hand, he was prepared to keep quiet on the matter whilst the Crusaders believed it was real. After all, they needed all the help they could get.

Just over three weeks after the Muslim army had settled down for a long siege, the gates were thrown open and the Crusaders emerged ready for battle. At their head was Adhemar de la Puy bearing the newly found Lance. The day ended with the rout of the Muslims – a day in which many of the Crusaders claimed they had seen St George, St Maurice and St Demetrius riding alongside them in battle. Clearly the genuine Lance had been found. Carried by a bishop, it had summoned the support of the saints and the Crusaders had won the day. Who could doubt it now?

A year later, in June 1099, the Christian army arrived at the gates of Jerusalem. According to an unknown chronicler of the attack on the city, the Crusaders' first attack was repelled and they 'were all surprised and alarmed'. Then a knight named Letholdus reached the top of the city's wall and drove the defenders back. More knights followed and soon the Crusaders were racing to the Temple of Solomon, killing anyone in their path. At this, the Muslim leader guarding the wall by the Tower of David opened the gates and admitted Count Raymond and his troops. Again, the Crusaders raced to the Temple, slaughtering indiscriminately as was the custom of victors against a city that had refused to surrender when under siege. When they arrived at the Temple they found 'a great crowd of pagans of

The Holy Lance held by Adhemar de la Puy in the defeat of the Muslim army before Antioch.

both sexes'. Appalled at the killing, Tancred, the King of Sicily, and Gaston de Beert sent forward their banners to hold over the crowd, thus saving their lives. There then followed a period of looting before the rampaging Crusaders 'went rejoicing and weeping for joy to adore the sepulchre of our Saviour Jesus and there discharged their debt to Him'.

Just over a week later, Lord Godfrey of Bouillon – who had sold his castle in Bouillon to the Bishop of Liège to raise funds for his Crusade – was elected the first Crusader ruler of Jerusalem. He never used the title 'king' in the belief that the only true king of Jerusalem was Christ himself.

2

QUEEN ELEANOR AND THE GRAIL

The 34-year-old Prince Raymond of Antioch bore many of the knightly attributes favoured by both men and women in the twelfth century. He was tall, handsome and gallant; his chronicler called him 'magnificent beyond measure'. He had also been very lucky. The youngest son of William IX, Duke of Aquitaine, Raymond had been sent as a boy from his home in Poitiers to serve at the English court. At the age of 21 he was summoned to the Holy Land by King Fulk of Jerusalem under conditions of great secrecy. As Regent of Antioch, following the death of Bohemund II in 1130, Fulk intended that Raymond should marry Constance, the 8-year-old daughter, only child and heiress of Bohemund. The problem with this arrangement was the child's mother, Alice, who lived with her daughter as Acting Regent in Antioch. Fulk handled this problem by having Raymond propose to Alice (who was still under 30 years old) and, as she was preparing for the wedding, marrying the young man to Constance behind her mother's back. Despite this unpromising start, the marriage proved to be a happy one (especially with the bride's mother removing herself from the scene in outrage).

Now Prince of Antioch, Raymond soon faced problems with the Byzantine emperor's continuous demands that Raymond hand the city and state over to him. With these demands either rebuffed or handled through diplomacy, Raymond then found himself facing a much more dangerous situation.

The Crusader state of Edessa, to the north of Antioch, fell to the Muslims in 1144. It was recaptured briefly in 1146, but was almost immediately lost yet again. When news of the loss of the Christian state reached Pope Eugenius III, the Pontiff called for a Crusade to evict the Muslims. In the beginning, the response was somewhat unenthusiastic. The monkish Louis VII of France had already made plans to go on a pilgrimage to Jerusalem in memory of his dead brother Phillip, and had to be persuaded by senior clergymen to go crusading instead. Eventually, he was to be joined by Conrad III of Germany and other Crusaders would come from Aquitaine, Brittany, Burgundy, Lorraine, Normandy and England.

In March 1148 Raymond was given a message that a Crusader army was just about to sail into the harbour of St Simeon, close to Antioch. Leaving immediately, he arrived at the port only to be met by a sight he had hoped never to see. The Crusaders were under the command of Louis, and they made a sorry sight. Weary, and worn down by constant Muslim harassment, their journey to Antioch had been a nightmare. Initially buoyed up by tales of a German victory ahead of them, they arrived at the scene of a battle only to find piles of putrid German corpses. Most of the baggage train had been lost when the rear of the army was attacked in later engagements with the Turks, and Louis himself, who had no apparent skills as a war leader, only just escaped death or capture when he fled from the Muslims and scrambled away by 'making use of some tree roots which God had provided for his safety'. There was, however, for Raymond at least, one bright aspect of Louis' arrival – the French king had brought his wife Eleanor, Raymond's niece.

Left: Louis VII of France and Queen Eleanor.

Below: Raymond of Poitiers welcoming Louis VII to Antioch.

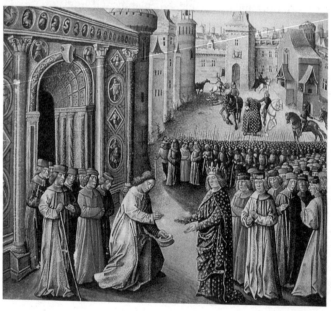

The beautiful and intelligent Eleanor of Aquitaine came from a considerably different background to her pious and frequently humourless husband. Her grandfather, William IX, had a mistress in the splendidly named Dangereuse, the wife of Aimeric I, Vicomte de Châtellerault, who also happened to be his daughter-in-law's mother. Using such methods as were available to her, Dangereuse had managed to arrange for her daughter, Aenor, to marry William's eldest son, also named William (and elder brother to Raymond). Eleanor was born of this union in 1122 and, although she had a younger brother – also named William – her mother and brother died, leaving her heiress to the lands of Aquitaine. These riches came to the 15-year-old when her father died whilst on a pilgrimage to Santiago de Compostela in April 1137. In his will, William had left the new Duchess of Aquitaine under the guardianship of King Louis VI, who rewarded such trust by sending his son, also Louis, to marry Eleanor, thus bringing Aquitaine into French possession.

For Eleanor, the next few years were enlivened by the usual squabbles with the Pope and minor wars with neighbouring states, until the call came from Pope Eugenius for a Crusade to be mounted for the reclamation of Edessa from the Muslims. Having initially fallen out with the hugely influential Abbot Bernard of Clairvaux, Eleanor swiftly changed tack and took up the Cross in front of the Abbot alongside her husband. They would go on Crusade together, leaving behind their year-old daughter, Marie.

Now at Antioch, and with the awful experiences of the journey behind her, Eleanor blossomed in the presence of her uncle. Friends from childhood (there were just a few years difference in their ages), they were frequently to be seen laughing and holding hands as they walked through the gardens of the palace whilst in animated conversation. Soon the gossipmongers were at work. Eleanor was not particularly popular with a number of the Crusaders as it was claimed that many of the losses to the Turks had been caused by the huge amount of baggage she had brought along whilst her own troops, the Aquitaines, were at the other end of the straggling column. Now they whispered into Louis' ear that 'she disregarded her marriage vows and was unfaithful to her husband'.

To this was added the further complication that Raymond wanted, and had expected, Louis to support him in an attempt to regain Edessa. To his and Eleanor's astonishment, Louis wished to do nothing more than go to Jerusalem and pray in the Church of the Holy Sepulchre. The French king had reverted from Crusader to pilgrim. When reasoned argument failed to change Louis' mind, Eleanor made a startling demand: she wanted her marriage annulled on the grounds of consanguinity. Louis and Eleanor were third cousins, once removed. Both had a common ancestor in Robert II of Normandy, Louis' great-great-grandfather. Her husband's prompt reaction was to remove his troops from Antioch and practically kidnap his own wife as she was physically man-handled away from Raymond's presence.

After Louis had completed his pilgrimage to Jerusalem, he agreed with Conrad of Germany and Baldwin of Jerusalem to launch an attack against the Syrian city of Damascus. Such an offensive bordered on the utterly pointless as the Emir of Damascus was keen to remain on friendly terms with the Europeans after having fallen out with the other Muslim leaders. As if to underline the folly of such a plan, the attack itself failed miserably when the Crusaders took themselves from a position of relative safety and sustenance, in the fruit orchards on the north-west side of the city, to an open position to the east of Damascus. There, with no food and water, the Crusaders' camp seethed with rumours of treachery. Divisions soon appeared in the leadership to the degree that Louis ordered the combined armies to retreat. As they fell back on Jerusalem, the Muslims launched attack after attack and many men died in the carnage, leaving 'the bodies stinking so powerfully that the birds almost fell out of the sky'.

For Eleanor, the disaster at Damascus did nothing but increase her contempt for Louis, who was showing an increasing reluctance to return to France to face the massing criticisms of his failure in the Holy Land. When, in the spring of 1149, they eventually sailed from Acre, their relationship had broken down to the extent that Louis and Eleanor sailed on different ships.

Following a failed attempt to capture the ships by a Greek force sent out by the Byzantine emperor, Eleanor and Louis lost sight of each other. For two months the Queen of France and Duchess of Aquitaine disappeared with, apparently, no one knowing her whereabouts. However, of all the places in the eastern Mediterranean, there is only one place for which she would have voluntarily bent her course – and that had to be Antioch.

Obviously, she would have looked forward to seeing her uncle once again. But there may have been much more to her return than a simple chance of seeing Prince Raymond. Returning to Antioch involved high stakes: she could have run up against Turkish ships on her approach and, even if she arrived safely, the Muslims could have launched an assault against the city and taken it. Raymond could already be captured or dead. So, if she did return to the city, why would she have taken these risks?

The Lance used to pierce Christ's side on the Cross had, only a few decades earlier, been found in St Peter's Cathedral. Although there was no mention in the Gospels of a cup being used to hold Christ's blood, and no record of a cup being found at Antioch, the two relics frequently accompany each other in subsequent art and literature. Could it be that Raymond had discovered the cup and had told Eleanor of his discovery during their walks in the palace gardens? If this was the case, Eleanor would not only have been aware of the great significance of the relic, but also of the risk of it falling into the hands of the

Muslims, as had happened to the True Cross at Jerusalem. As subsequent events were to show, the possibility of Eleanor returning to obtain the cup is raised to the highly probable.

If Eleanor did visit Antioch, Raymond seems to have, to all intents and purposes, committed suicide within a few days of her departure. Taking a force of less than 2,000 knights and footmen, and linking up with Hashshashin (Assassin) forces, Raymond left for the city of Inab, which was under siege by the Muslims. On his approach, the Turks raised the siege and withdrew. Then, much to the astonishment of the Turkish commanders, Raymond took his forces away from the protection of the city and led them on to an open plain. At first, the Muslims assumed that he was expecting reinforcements, but, when none appeared, they surrounded the men from Antioch and their allies. The next day, the 7,000 Turks, mainly made up of cavalry, attacked. By the end of the engagement, along with the majority of his troops, Raymond was dead. His head was cut off and sent as a gift to the Caliph of Baghdad. For a prince raised in the art of warfare, it had been an extraordinarily inept action and the chroniclers could only assume that he was 'wearied by killing and exhausted in spirit'.

He may also have been anything from dejected to elated by the thought that a priceless holy relic had been saved and was safely on its way to Christian Europe.

3

THE ANGEVIN ASCENT

If it is assumed that Eleanor *did* obtain the precious relic from Raymond, it certainly did not bring her immediate relief from her marital sufferings. Despite her pleading that the marriage had clearly displeased God and had resulted in no male heirs, the Pope not only refused the annulment, but provided a chamber and a bed for Eleanor and Louis to restart their marriage. This enforced second honeymoon saw Eleanor become pregnant again, giving birth to yet another daughter, Alice. Now even Louis was beginning to suspect that God was displeased.

In August 1151 the French court was visited by Geoffrey, Duke of Anjou and Maine, and his wife, Matilda, the only surviving child of Henry I of England. On the death of her father, Matilda had been outmanoeuvred by her cousin Stephen of Blois – a grandson of William the Conqueror. Stephen had crowned himself King of England and settled down to a life of deteriorating relations with his barons. Four years later, during a time when 'Christ and His angels slept', Geoffrey and Matilda invaded England and Stephen was captured at the battle of Lincoln. The triumph was short-lived, for Matilda's half-brother, Robert of Gloucester, was captured by Stephen's troops and she was forced to hand over her royal prisoner in order to get Robert back. Eventually, Matilda returned to Normandy and, at the time of the visit to Paris, the Crown of England was still in dispute with no resolution in sight beyond a return to civil war.

Such matters would have concerned Eleanor little. She knew that Louis' true sympathies lay with Stephen, and probably knew that her husband had been carrying out a desultory border war against Normandy for some months in support of the King of England. But what *would* have concerned the 29-year-old queen greatly was Geoffrey and Matilda's 18-year-old son Henry, Duke of Normandy.

Henry was not entirely unknown in the court of France. At one time, he had been considered as a possible husband for Louis and Eleanor's daughter, Marie. But that idea had been dismissed on the insistence of church leaders who noted that Eleanor's mother and Henry were related to the third degree. Such a consideration, however, did not stop Eleanor herself looking at the strapping young duke with more than a passing interest. With the possibility of her marriage being annulled in the near future, she had no intention of retiring behind the cold grey walls of a convent.

Clearly, at some stage in the visit, Henry and Eleanor had contrived to meet. The still-beautiful queen and the handsome, battle-hardened duke soon came to an understanding – with the annulment out of the way, they would marry. There was, however, a possible complication. According to a leading chronicler of the time, Gerald of Wales, Geoffrey, Henry's father, had 'carnally known Queen Eleanor' when he had served at the French court. The problem, if it existed, was much reduced when Geoffrey died of a fever the following month. Then, at last, in March 1152, Louis and Eleanor were divorced, and Aquitaine was returned with the former queen.

Eleanor lost no time in returning to her beloved ancestral home at Poitiers. But the journey had been fraught with danger. On the first day of her travels, she learned that an attempt to capture her was to be mounted that night by

Theobald of Blois, the nephew of King Stephen. Taking evasive action, she learned a few days later that another attempt would be made against her, this time by Geoffrey, the 17-year-old brother of Henry. Once again she side-stepped the danger and arrived home safely. In the meantime, she made sure that Henry knew of her divorce and, within weeks, the Duke of Normandy arrived at Poitiers. They were married on 18 May 1152, just two months after her divorce from Louis. Four months later, a son, William, was born.

In the cold, damp, early days of January 1153, Henry landed at Bristol with over 3,000 men and captured Malmesbury Castle. Shortly afterwards, he faced Stephen's army across the River Avon. As the two armies prepared for battle, the heavens opened and heavy rain descended, blown by a sharp wind into the faces of Stephen's troops. The king, wearied and uncomfortable, surrendered the field to Henry by simply leaving it. Henry turned his attention to Wallingford in Oxfordshire, where Stephen was besieging some of his supporters. The king, as he approached Henry's forces, fell – or was thrown – from his horse three times. Badly shaken, he agreed to meet Henry in private. What was said is not known, but Stephen returned, not only to call off the battle, but also to raise the siege. Prince Eustace, the sole heir to the Crown, was enraged at this turn of events and stormed off to plunder the Abbey of Bury St Edmunds. As he waited in a nearby castle for his troops to bring in the plunder, he dined on a meal of eels. Within minutes he was dead.

Left with no heir, Stephen met Henry at Winchester and came to a compromise – later confirmed by the leaders among the earls and barons in London. Stephen would continue to reign, but would declare that Henry was to be his successor. It was not to be a long wait. Just nine months after the treaty had been signed, Stephen was dead and Eleanor, Duchess of Aquitaine, and possessor of the cup that was believed to have caught the blood of Christ as He died on the Cross, was Queen of England.

Henry II proved to be a good king to his people, but was not so successful in the question of family matters. A tough fighter and forceful leader, who preferred plain dress to kingly raiment, Henry was also able to delegate to trusted officials who could run the machinery of government in his absence. He made significant changes to the legal system, which resulted in the introduction of a body of common law, and weakened the feudal system by demanding monetary payment in lieu of military service. The marriage of Henry and Eleanor produced eight children, all of whom, with the exception of William, who died aged 3, survived into adulthood. Henry, however, was also a womaniser of heroic proportions who thought nothing of bringing at least one of his bastard children into the royal household – against the wishes of his wife.

By 1157, Eleanor found she had much more to contend with than her husband's infidelity. Henry had turned to the Archbishop of Canterbury for advice in the matter of a new chancellor, a role of huge importance as the new office holder would become the keeper of the Great Seal of the Kingdom and be responsible for all new charters signed by the king. Effectively, with the exception of the royal family and the Church, the chancellor would be the most powerful person in the land. The archbishop, Theobald, had no hesitation in recommending his highly talented, but unordained, archdeacon – Thomas Becket.

It did not take long for Henry and Becket to realise they were cast from a similar mould. Soon the king and the chancellor were to be seen hunting together. They drank together, whored together, played jokes together and laughed uproariously at each other's riotous behaviour. In a remarkably short time, Becket, a merchant's son, took on all the attributes of a noble lord. In matters of dress, he far outshone the king, and his house – paid for by the king – became a byword for ostentatious taste and luxury. When it was decided that the king's eldest surviving son, a 3-year-old also named Henry, should marry Marguerite, the 1-year-old daughter of Eleanor's first husband, Becket was the obvious person to send to carry out the negotiations. Of course, the intended bride and groom were far too young to marry immediately, but the earlier the contract was established the better. Becket rose to the occasion in spectacular manner. He arrived at Paris with a huge retinue of knights, squires, clerks and stewards as hundreds of foot soldiers sang songs at the head of the parade. Eight wagons carried his personal goods, whilst another two were loaded with English ale. Hunting dogs ran at the heels of Becket's men, many of whom carried hawks on their wrists. So effective was this display of wealth and power that Becket not only returned with a contract for the marriage of Henry and Marguerite, but another for the future marriage of Louis' daughter Alice to Richard, the second eldest child of Henry and Eleanor.

Little of this, apart from the political implications, brought any joy to Eleanor's heart. From being first in the king's affections, she had been rapidly relegated to a sullen background by a tradesman's son who saw much more of her husband than she did. In revenge, she did what many women have done over the ages – she spent a lot of money. She spent £22 13s 2d on renovating her private quarters, her chapel and her garden, and on the transport of her personal wine, incense and baggage. She awarded herself £226 from the Treasury, as well as £56 for 5-year-old Prince Henry. In September 1160, Henry II's court records note: '*Et pro ii unciis auri ad deaurandas cuppas Regis 2 marcas argent.*' – 'And two silver marks for two ounces of gold to gild over the small royal vessels.' This does not mean, of course, that amongst the 'small vessels' that Eleanor had gilded on this occasion was the ancient silver cup in the form of a chalice that she had obtained from her uncle, Prince Raymond of Antioch. It does show, however, that such an activity was not only known about, but was actually undertaken by the queen.

4

THE BECKET CHALLENGE

On 18 April 1161, Theobald, the Archbishop of Canterbury, died. It took a year before Henry decided on a replacement. And who could be better than his compliant friend, Thomas Becket? By combining the post of chancellor with that of the archbishop – a precedent already set by the Archbishop of Cologne being the chancellor to the Holy Roman Emperor – Henry could provide himself with a conduit to the wealth of the Church. After all, as chancellor, Becket had forced a heavy tax upon the Church in England, amongst others, to pay for an attack against Toulouse. Furthermore, with Becket as archbishop, Henry would have a supportive barrier against papal interference in affairs of state – one affair in particular. Following the pattern established by both the Holy Roman Emperor and the previous King of France, Henry intended to secure the succession of his Crown by having his eldest son, Henry, crowned as king whilst he, the reigning monarch, was still on the throne. Just over a decade earlier, King Stephen had tried to have his son, Eustace, crowned, but the then archbishop, Theobald, and the Pope had refused permission. Becket, the king's old friend, would never countenance such opposition, and Henry's concerns over the succession would be set at rest.

Although Becket had served as provost at Beverley Minster, as a canon at both Lincoln and St Paul's Cathedrals and as archdeacon at Canterbury, he had never been accepted into the Church as a priest. Consequently, on Saturday 2 June 1162, Thomas Becket was ordained as a priest. The next morning, he was consecrated as a bishop and, in the afternoon of the same day, made Archbishop of Canterbury.

Just a few weeks were to pass before Henry, who had remained in Normandy during Becket's enthronement, began to wonder if he had made a mistake in making his friend archbishop. A messenger arrived with a package for the king. On opening it, Henry found himself looking at the Great Seal of England – Becket had resigned the post of chancellor.

From that moment on, the relationship between the king and Becket rapidly fell apart. Testing the waters, Henry demanded that the archbishop give up his privileges of appointing his own archdeacon and of awarding other posts within the clergy. Becket not only refused, but took back land and property that had once belonged to Canterbury and had been distributed among friends of the king. At this, Henry played a royal card – he demanded that a traditional payment to local sheriffs be re-directed as a substantial contribution from the Church to his own treasury. Despite it being a clear challenge to the previously undisputed right of the king to demand arbitrary taxes, Becket refused. Then the conflict took on a personal note. Henry had decided that his youngest brother, the mild-mannered and unambitious William, should marry the widowed Countess de Warenne. On her father's death the widow would inherit the earldom of Surrey, a substantial inheritance that would take care of William's future. Such an arrangement, however, needed the agreement of the Archbishop of Canterbury. Again, Becket refused. By now, angry and exasperated, Henry was left with few options. He would tackle the Church directly.

With the increase in power of the Christian Church since the time of William the Conqueror, it had assumed for itself the right to try all criminal acts committed by its clergy in its own courts. In the beginning, this system caused few problems as the numbers of clergy involved was small, and the Church attracted few law-breakers. However, with the introduction of lay clergy, the numbers had grown out of all proportion and many crimes, some of great seriousness, were being dealt with in the Church's own courts – and it had not gone unnoticed that these courts were extremely lenient when handing out punishments, even for the most serious of crimes. Since Henry had come to the throne, over a hundred murders had been committed with the perpetrators escaping punishment through their appearance in the Church courts.

There was one interesting exception to the mild punishments meted out by the Church courts. A clergyman was charged and found guilty of stealing from the church of St Mary-le-Bow in Cheapside, London. Extraordinarily, Becket had the man branded – a punishment condemned by the Church's own law for, as all men were created 'in the image of God', to deliberately defile that image was to defy God. The branding is usually explained to be an attempt by Becket to persuade the king that secular trial of the clergy was unnecessary as more severe punishments were to be handed out in the Church courts. It is more likely, however, that Henry was being sent a message. The item stolen by the clergyman was a chalice.

Matters eventually came to a head when Philip de Brois, a canon of Bedford Cathedral, murdered a knight. After facing a trial in the Bishop of Lincoln's court, de Brois was acquitted on the grounds that he swore he was innocent and could find others who would also swear the same on his behalf. Such a verdict did not impress the sheriff of Bedford who tried to have de Brois brought before a secular court. This was met by de Brois personally and publicly rounding on the sheriff with a vicious tirade. Becket's response was to send de Brois away with a mild banishment. Word, however, had reached the Pope who, not wishing to lose the support of Henry against the papal enemies, appealed to Becket to agree to the king's demands. After listening to the advice of others in the Church, the archbishop finally agreed.

Shortly afterwards, in January 1164, Henry called a meeting with the archbishops and bishops to underline the agreement. The Council of Clarendon, held in the presence of the great barons and earls of the country, was used by the king to announce a series of sixteen articles (the Constitutions of Clarendon) which would establish the legal positions of Church and State. Even before the articles were introduced, when asked to swear to the customs of the realm without any exceptions, Becket refused. After three days of heated debate, Henry brought out the written constitutions, the third of which stated that if a member of the clergy was charged with an offence, he would be put before a Church court; if found guilty, the cleric would then face a secular court. Despite the glaring loophole that would encourage the Church courts to find all offenders not guilty, in order to avoid the involvement of the secular courts, Becket refused to accept the constitution. After further debate, in which Becket began to become more isolated, something caused him to change his mind. As if exasperated, the archbishop suddenly told the other clergy that they should agree to the constitutions and make their oaths accordingly – as he would. But once the oaths had been taken, including his own, Becket made great play of publicly regretting having agreed to Henry's demands.

Outraged by Becket's withdrawal of support for the consti-tutions, Henry was dealt a further blow when his 27-year-old brother William died. William, it was rumoured, had died of a broken heart caused by Becket's refusal to grant permission for his marriage to the Countess de Warenne. Once again, the king launched an assault upon his obstinate archbishop.

In late September, 1164, a charge of contempt was brought against the archbishop by John FitzGilbert, the hereditary Marshal of England. Becket was fined £500. This was followed by an examination of the accounts during his time as chancellor. In turn, this led to a demand that the archbishop present himself, in the company of other senior clergymen, at Northampton Castle. Becket arrived on 6 October, under the impression that he was to be made to answer for the charge of contempt. To his utter shock, the archbishop found that he had, in fact, been summoned to face charges of alleged misuse of funds that had passed through his hands when he was chancellor. In all, the king claimed that Becket had misappropriated the huge sum of 40,000 marks – over £26,000. Refusing to accept the charges, and any subsequent verdict, the archbishop stormed out of the room and ran into shouted abuse delivered by Ranulf de Broc – the splendidly titled 'Doorkeeper of the King's chambers and Keeper of the Royal Whores'. Becket loudly reminded de Broc that one of the knight's family had been hanged before angrily striding from the building. Outmanoeuvred by Henry, Becket stole away in the middle of the night. He made his way to Lincoln where he spent a night before sailing down the River Witham to the port of Boston. Continuing his way down the coast, the archbishop arrived at Sandwich and crossed over to Flanders. He and his small party then rode for France where he sought the aid of the Pope, Alexander III, who at that time was residing close to Paris. The archbishop was soon to be followed by many of his extended family, hounded out of the country under the king's authority by Ranulf de Broc. De Broc was awarded Saltwood Castle for his work, one of the archbishop's properties directly south of Canterbury along the old Roman road and close to the coastal town of Hythe. Less than two years later, whilst preaching in the abbey at Vézelay, Becket surprised no one by excommunicating – amongst others – Ranulf de Broc.

There remains, however, something that appears to be unspoken in this trail of conflict. With his constant refusal to agree to any of Henry's demands, which ranged from the acquisition of land and the refusal to pay taxes to a modest change in the law, and the personal affront to Henry over William's intended marriage, it is as if Becket had been making stipulations of his own. And, when his orders were not met, he had retaliated by obstructing Henry's attempt to rule. Becket's chronicler, William of Newbury, writing in around 1200, was baffled by the archbishop's apparently pointless intransigence 'because no benefit would result therefrom'. The words 'extortion' and 'blackmail' had yet to be coined, but there is a strong possibility that Becket was trying to obtain something from Henry.

The most prestigious objects that could be owned by the Church were relics. One that could be linked directly to Christ would be held in higher esteem than all others. Splinters of the True Cross were held in costly reliquaries throughout Christendom. Other valuable caskets and crystal boxes held single thorns from the Crown of Thorns and many Crucifixion Nails were held in heartfelt adoration. At least three Lances were known to exist, each defended vigorously as the genuine item. In a bizarre twist of fate, after his death, Becket himself was to be subjected to the insatiable desire to obtain relics.

Archbishop Thomas Becket
argues with the king.

Having once been so close to the king, it would have been extremely unlikely for Becket to have been unaware that Eleanor owned a chalice that was claimed to be the vessel used to hold the blood of Christ. For a church to be the holder of such a remarkable relic would have been truly sensational, and would have attracted pilgrims from throughout Christendom. Becket knew that there was only one place for the chalice – and that had to be in his possession, at Canterbury Cathedral.

Eleanor, on the other hand, would never have handed over the relic, no matter how sacred, to the upstart merchant's son now turned renegade, who was putting pressure on her husband in an attempt to seize it. With Becket having fled the country, she could get closer to her husband. It was not long before she was pregnant with her seventh child by Henry, and he made her Regent of Anjou and Maine whilst he went off to war against the Welsh. But, if Eleanor thought that Becket had given up hope of obtaining the chalice, she was mistaken.

In May 1165 she crossed the Channel to visit Angers, the centre of her new regency. Whilst there, she met her mother's brother, Ralph de Faye, who, eleven years earlier, she had appointed to look after her interests in Aquitaine. As de Faye informed Eleanor of matters current in her duchy, she received another, less welcome party. A delegation arrived from none other than Archbishop Becket, now in residence in Burgundy at the Abbey of Pontigny. What was discussed between them and the queen is not known, but it is not beyond the bounds of possibility that they pointed out to her the benefits that would be obtained by handing over the chalice that Becket so eagerly sought. With the vessel in his hands, there would be no reason for conflict, no reason to oppose all that Henry wanted, both nationally and personally, and a perfect harmony would exist between State and Church. They left empty-handed. Shortly afterwards, Becket received a letter from the Bishop of Poitiers informing him that Eleanor and de Faye were seen to be closer to each other than might be considered proper, giving rise to 'conjectures which grow day by day and which seem to deserve credence'. Was this yet another attempt to find evidence that could be used in an endeavour to extort the chalice, this time against Eleanor herself? If it was, the attempt failed again, perhaps because Eleanor was soon occupied with other matters.

Her contact with Henry was brief over the following months, but long enough for her to become pregnant with his eighth child. By now, however, such intimacies were little more than a duty on the king's part to ensure the continuation of the Crown, and Eleanor soon discovered that his failed war against the Welsh had achieved, for Henry at least, a charming distraction. Whilst fighting in Wales, the king had met and become besotted with Rosamond de Clifford – the 'Fair Rosamond'.

Although the king had previously had mistresses, the affair with Rosamond was clearly of a different order. Markedly different to Eleanor, the king's new love was a beautiful young woman; placid, compliant and without ambition beyond being an ornament at Henry's side. After the birth of her latest child, John, Eleanor left England and set up her court at Poitiers, the capital of her beloved Aquitaine. Her leaving seems to have left Henry unmoved, since he clearly preferred the delights of Rosamond to the pursuit of his ageing wife.

The embittered Queen of England not only deserted her errant husband, but carried out an act that would strike at both the king and the detested Becket. One wanted the gilded chalice for his ecclesiastical prestige; the other would put it at risk for a quieter life in the arms of Rosamond. Instead, Eleanor decided that she would put the relic into the protection of the one group who owed no loyalty to her husband, and to none in the Church except the Pope himself. She would place the chalice under the protection of the Order of the Poor Knights of Christ and the Temple of Solomon – better known to history as the Knights Templar.

5

THE TEMPLAR RESPONSE

The origins of the Knights Templar are veiled in mystery. From what little is known it may, with reasonable safety, be suggested that in 1113 nine knights, headed by Hughes de Payens, took vows of poverty, chastity and obedience before the Patriarch of Jerusalem. They thereupon dedicated themselves as Poor Soldiers of Christ with the mission of protecting pilgrims as they made their way to the holy sites of Jerusalem.

With the capture of the Holy City, most of the Crusaders had returned to their homes in Europe. The succeeding waves of pilgrims, however, faced constant attacks from Muslim raiding parties or ambushes. Many of the unarmed pilgrims lost their lives as they were robbed and physically injured in these assaults.

It is difficult to see how just nine knights could have defended the large number of pilgrims arriving in the Holy Land. In all probability, the only practical method would have been to have acted as escorts from the port of Jaffa, over the 40 miles of rocky road to Jerusalem. Whatever method was used, the knights made such an impression that when King Baldwin II succeeded to the throne in 1118 (Godfrey of Bouillon's reservation about using the title 'king' was soon dropped by his descendants), they were given quarters in the eastern part of the king's palace, built on the supposed site of King Solomon's temple. Nearby stables were donated by the canons of the Holy Sepulchre for the knights' horses. Just a few hundred yards away reared the glittering gold dome of the former al-Aqsa mosque – now redesignated as a Christian church under the name of the Temple of the Lord.

For the following nine years, the knights carried out their work guarding the pilgrims. Remaining faithful to their monastic vows, they were fed and clothed by a combination of the king, the Patriarch and the canons of the Holy Sepulchre. It is during this time that rumour, myth and legend have the knights burrowing beneath their quarters into the forgotten vaults of the Temple of Solomon in search of some mysterious object or objects. Only the very slightest of evidence remains to suggest any truth in this idea, and it is unlikely that the knights, dedicated to the unshakeable truth of the 'New Law' (New Testament) at the expense of the 'Old Law' (Old Testament), would have searched for anything from before the time of Christ. Even if anything was found, it was likely to be unimpressive as, by 1127, the knights were becoming somewhat disillusioned and were desperate for help from beyond the walls of Jerusalem. That year, Hughes de Payens and other knights left for Europe to plead their cause.

De Payens was a minor member of the House of Champagne (the Count of Champagne had been an early supporter of the Poor Soldiers of Christ), so he made his way to Troyes, the leading city in that region. In 1128 a council was held at Troyes to discuss disputes within the Church. The council was chaired by the Pope's representative, Cardinal Matthew, and attended by many senior figures in the Church, including the council secretary, Abbot Bernard of Clairvaux.

The abbot, a member of the ruling class in Burgundy (closely allied to the House of Champagne), was a remarkable man by any measure. In 1113, at the age of 23, Bernard turned up at the Abbey of Citeaux and asked the abbot, an Englishman named

Stephen Harding, to accept him and the thirty young noblemen he had brought with him as monks. Abbot Stephen would have been delighted, as the abbey had only recently been founded in response to the Benedictine decline from the rigorous monastic life to a more indulgent lifestyle. The monks of Citeaux had become known as Cistercians and wore white robes to contrast with the black robes of the Benedictines. After just three years, Bernard was sent to establish a new abbey at Clairvaux. Before long, Bernard was having so many applicants to join him at Clairvaux that he was forced to establish new Cistercian abbeys in France, eventually spreading the Order throughout much of the rest of Europe. When Bernard and de Payens met at the Council of Troyes, it was soon clear that the knight's search for support had found fertile ground in the abbot.

Throughout the feudal period, the military and the Church kept each other at arm's length. Knights and soldiers were seen by the Church as little more than oafish thugs whose only method of advancing their cause was by a brutal force of arms. Clerics, on the other hand, were seen by the knights as pampered parasites who had done nothing but pray or plant vegetables for their privileges. Now, in the Poor Soldiers of Christ, Bernard could see a bridge between knights and clergy. Here, in fact, were knights who had bound themselves by monastic vows and whose enemies were the very enemies of Christ and His Church. Not only that, they were also based on the very site of King Solomon's temple. Bernard gave his support readily and, in response to a request by de Payens (already referred to as 'Master' of the Order), produced a list of rules by which the newly named Order of the Poor Knights of Christ and the Temple of Solomon would conduct their lives.

The knights were enjoined to be pure of heart and obedient; they had to be persevering and diligent and had to defend the poor and the weak. Church had to be attended and prayers said where possible. All the brethren in a 'Chapter' would decide on the acceptance of a new brother and excommunicated knights could be allowed into the Order with the permission of a bishop. Prayers could be offered whilst seated, but not so loud as to disturb others in their prayers. The knights were to wear white mantles that were to be without decoration, but of good fit. The old mantles of the knights were to be handed to their squires and sergeants (non-knight combatants attached to the Order), but only after being dyed black. Shirts and bed linen could be possessed by the knights and others, and shirts, breeches, shoes and belts were to be worn in bed. Their hair was to be kept short, as were their beards and moustaches. To a background of the reading of Holy Scripture, the knights were to eat in pairs to ensure that no knight indulged in fasting or any other monastic form of abstinence. The meal was to be eaten in silence; if speaking was necessary it was to be done in a quiet voice. Meat was to be eaten no more than three times a week, but knights, chaplains and clerks were allowed two meat meals on Sundays; sergeants and squires just one. After evening prayers, a silence was to be kept except in cases of emergency. The sick and elderly were to be nursed by all the brethren; the Master was to be obeyed in all things and advice was to be sought only from the wise. No lockable container was allowed without permission, no letters were allowed to be received unless by permission and then the letter had to be read to the recipient. Gifts were only to be accepted by permission of the Master. Self-declared faults were to be treated leniently, but pride, boastfulness and self-promotion could lead to dismissal from the Order. The knights were allowed up to three horses with plain saddlery equipment and one squire, and if the squire behaved himself, he was not to be beaten. Hunting was forbidden, except for lions, which were considered an appropriate prey for the Templars. Tithes intended for the Church could be received with the local bishop's permission. Killing the enemies of Christ was deemed not a sin. Knights were to see their own death as vengeance for the death of Christ, and be ready to render up their souls for the sake of their brethren. Dead knights were to be remembered by giving the food they would have eaten to a poor person for forty days. Secular knights, or 'Confreres' (knights who had not taken the monastic vows), were allowed to be attached to the Order. They could not live with the brother-knights, nor could they wear the white mantle. If a confrere died whilst serving with the Templars, a pauper was to be fed for seven days in the knight's memory. Squires and sergeants were to be allowed to serve for a fixed period if that was their wish. Married knights could become brothers, but could not wear a white mantle; women could be financial supporters, but not members of the Order, and no knight could embrace or kiss a woman.

The following year, Bernard wrote to de Payens a letter which became known by the title 'In Praise of the New Knighthood'. In it, the abbot lays down his idea of what a Knight Templar should be: he should be 'a truly fearless knight, protected on all sides, for his soul is protected by the armour of faith as his body is protected by the armour of steel'. The warriors of the new Order were urged to 'go boldly, you knights, and repel the enemies of the Cross with a gallant heart. Know that neither death nor life can take from you the love of God which is in Jesus Christ. In the face of peril repeat "Whether we live or die, we are the Lord's".' For the knights 'to inflict death or to die for Christ is no sin, instead it is a justified claim for glory'. Yet again, Bernard stressed the guarantee of deliverance, either physically or spiritually:

> The Knight of Christ may strike boldly, and die even more boldly, for he serves Christ when he strikes, and serves himself when he falls. He does not bear the sword in vain, for he is a Minister of God, serving to punish the evildoer and to praise the virtuous. If he kills an evildoer, he is not a murderer, but a slayer of evil.

This combination of personal duty, rigid ideals and soaring inspiration struck a righteous chord in knights throughout Christendom. So many applied for membership of the Order that Templar provinces rose up in France, England, Scotland, Portugal, Poitiers, Apulia, Hungary and Aragon. An order of ranking rapidly evolved with the Grand Master at its head. He was assisted in the administrative affairs by the Seneschal. The Marshal looked after military matters, with an Under Marshal who had particular responsibility for foot soldiers and stores.

The Standard Bearer had charge of the squires, whilst the Draper was accountable for the standard of dress of the Knights Templar. Commanders looked after Templar property and Provincial Masters looked after the western provinces. In addition, there existed a number of Templar fraternities made up of associate or lay brethren known as 'Brothers of the Temple'. These brethren achieved their status by supporting the Knights Templar either by regular donations or by serving alongside them as secular knights. Often these lay brethren would fully assume the white mantle of the Knights Templar on their death bed, or were clothed in one after death.

In 1139 the Pope, Innocent II, declared that the Knights Templar, regardless of nationality, were to owe loyalty to no one other than the Pope himself. They would not have to pay taxes or tithes, which caused anger amongst the clergy who saw the Templars as gaining benefits to their disadvantage. An example of this was that when a bishop decided one of his congregations had failed in some matter, he could put an 'interdiction' on the particular parish, requiring that the church be closed. This meant that baptisms, weddings and funerals could not be carried out. However, any Knight Templar – owing no loyalty to the bishop – could (no doubt for an appropriate donation) open up the church and let the required ceremony go ahead.

Pope Eugenius, a former Cistercian monk who had been trained under Bernard of Clairvaux, granted the Knights

Templar the right to use a red cross on their white mantles and shields in 1146. The red cross was to represent Christ's blood against the white of innocence and symbolised martyrdom. This produced the problem that many Crusaders used a shield bearing a red cross, until changes were made in 1188. To deal with this difficulty, the Knights Templar adopted a battle-shield of white with a wide black bar running horizontally along the top.

The Templar battle-shield reflected their battle-flag – again, white beneath an equal black area – to which they had given the name '*beauseant*' (probably with a meaning similar to 'piebald'). In battle, the Templars acted as shock troops whose main task was to punch a hole in the enemy line. Lined up stirrup to stirrup, ready to go into battle, the knights would sing the first verse of Psalm 115: '*Non nobis, Domine, non nobis, sed Nomini Tuo ad gloriam.*' – 'Not for us, Lord, not for us, but to Thy name give Glory.' The battle-flag would then be raised and greeted with a shout of '*Beauseant!*' and, often under the leadership of the Grand Master himself, the charge would begin with the knights remaining silent throughout. To the enemy, the sight of a tightly disciplined force of knights, packed together for maximum effect and coming straight at his part of the line with lances levelled, with only the sound of thundering hooves and jingling iron fittings, would have had an extremely impressive effect.

The Bishop of Acre, who frequently escorted the Templars in the field, said of them:

> When summoned to arms, they never demand the number of the enemy, but where are they? Lions they are in war, gentle as lambs in the monastery; fierce soldiers in the field, hermits and monks in religion; to the enemies of Christ ferocious and inexorable, but to Christians kind and gracious. They carry before them to battle, a banner, black at the top and white beneath, which they call Beauseant, that is to say, in the Gallic tongue, Bien-seant, because they are fair and favourable to the friends of Christ, but black and terrible to His enemies.

The Templars were the first to enter the battlefield and the last to leave it. No knight would leave the field whilst a single Templar battle-flag flew and, generally, if no battle-flag remained flying, no Templar was left alive. If a Templar was captured, unlike other Crusader knights, he could not hope to avoid death. Whereas the other knights could plead for an opportunity to raise a ransom, or surrender themselves to a life of slavery, the Saracens (as the Muslims were by now known) knew that the Templars had no private wealth of their own and those captured were instantly put to the sword. This was Templar warfare and the enemy felt it, not just in the Holy Land, but also in Spain, Cyprus and Portugal.

Astonishingly, there was another side to the Templars which is unlikely to have been foreseen by de Payens and his small group as they first arrived at Jerusalem.

Admirers, including royalty and noble families, showered the new Order with wealth beyond their imagining. Examples from England alone give some idea of the funds that were sent. Between them, King Stephen and Queen Matilda gave the Order the manors of Cressynge (including the church), Eagle, Cowley and Witham. They also gave two Oxfordshire mills, pasture in Shotover Forest and the church at Stretton in Rutland. The battle-scarred warrior Roger de Mowbray, who had fought alongside the Templars in the Second Crusade, was so impressed with their valour that, on his return to England, he gave them the manors of Kileby and Witheley, land on the Isle of Axholme, the Warwickshire town of Balshall and lands in Yorkshire. William, Lord Ashby, gave lands in Lincolnshire on which the Temple Bruer Preceptory was to be built (a preceptory was a Templar religious house and community subject to a provincial temple). Other notables who gave land and property included William Marshal, the Earl of Pembroke and his two sons; the Earls of Hereford, Devon, Cornwall, Northampton and Leicester; the Countess of Warwick; the Archbishop of York; the Dean of Lincoln Cathedral and the King of Scotland. The de Hastings family gave land at Wyxham and Hurst – the latter becoming the Templar preceptory known as Temple Hurst. Richard de Hastings was the Provincial Master for England on the accession of Henry II and had personally pleaded with Becket to accept the Clarendon Constitutions. His plea was brutally snubbed. William, the much loved younger brother of Henry II, who had died (it is said) of a broken heart when Becket refused permission for him to marry, gave the Templars land in the village of Ewell – later to become the preceptory, Temple Ewell. The archbishop, like many of his fellow priests, considered the Templars pseudo-clerics whose existence prevented much wealth from reaching the established Church, despite their support by the Pope. Henry II, the one-time friend and later ardent enemy of Becket, loaded the Templars with gifts including land around the Fleet river in London, the church of St Clement in the same city, several other churches including three in Lincolnshire, three manors, a park, a mill, the profits from the market at Witham, a fair at Temple Bruer, income from Irish property and three 'fat bucks' annually from the forests of Essex or Windsor.

In Provence, the acquisition of property began as early as 1130, when a Commandery (regional headquarters) was granted at Arles by King James I of Aragon. A hundred and fifty years later, the Order owned twenty-nine Commanderies and over a thousand farms.

All this, and much more land and property acquired throughout Europe, was not simply accepted as some form of tribute to be hoarded. Instead, the knights applied a significant level of business acumen to their donations and rapidly proved themselves to be entrepreneurs of the first order. Before long, they had so much wealth that they could afford to support sovereigns with loans. After the chaotic attempt to take Damascus during the Second Crusade, Louis VII, then the husband of Eleanor of Aquitaine, wrote to his vice-regent, Abbot Suger of St Denis, about the aid he had been given by the Templars:

> I cannot imagine how we could have subsisted for even the smallest space of time if it had not been for their support and assistance, which never failed me from the first day I set foot in these lands up to the time of my dispatching this letter – a succour ably afforded and generously persevered in. I therefore earnestly beseech you, that as these Brothers of the Temple have hitherto been blessed with the love of God, so now they may be gladdened and sustained by our love and favour. I have to inform you that they have lent me a considerable sum of money, which must be repaid to them quickly, that their house may not suffer, and that I may keep my word.

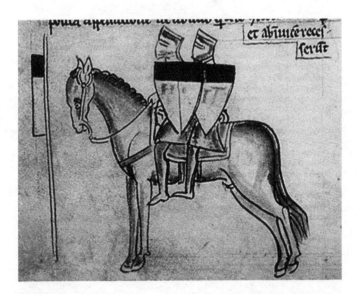

Two Knights Templar sharing a horse (as was illustrated on the Templar seal). Both are carrying the Templar battle-shield. To the left of them is the Templar battle-flag 'Beauseant'. (Illustration by Matthew Paris, c.1250)

Jacques de Maille, a Templar Marshal, fights to the death. (A Gustave Doré illustration)

Great Templar treasuries were established in Paris and London. Nobles travelling to the Crusades could deposit their treasures in the knowledge that they would be in safe hands until their return. Kings put their Crown jewels into the Templar treasuries and freely applied to the knights for loans in order to carry out Crusades or other minor war campaigns. Merchants and others travelling abroad could deposit large sums of money with the Templars and be issued with a promissory note, which could be used at a Templar establishment at their destination to retrieve the funds, thus doing away with the risk of being robbed en route. The charges placed against these services helped to considerably increase the wealth of the Templars.

It was not just expensive worldly goods that the Templars welcomed in their treasuries. They also found space for holy relics. It is widely believed and reported that they held a version of the Crown of Thorns, a piece of the True Cross, the martyred body of St Euphemia of Chalcedon and, possibly, the shroud in which Christ was buried (which certainly ended up in the possession of a Templar's family). It does not take much imagining to accept that the English Knights Templar would have been delighted with a request from the Queen of England to guard the chalice that may have been used by Christ at the Last Supper and, equally, may have been used to catch His blood as He died on the Cross. If Eleanor believed the relic to be genuine, and the Archbishop of Canterbury was desperate to get his hands on it, why should the Templars doubt it? And Eleanor knew that the relic would be safe, for the Templars would never release the item, except to the person who had presented it.

Six years after his flight from England, Becket had lost none of his calculating menace. He professed outrage at the crowning of the king's son, Prince Henry – now known as the Young King Henry – in June 1170. After demanding the permission from the Pope to excommunicate those clerics who had taken part in the ceremony (granted only to be used with discretion), he had attended a meeting with the king. Henry had been threatened with excommunication by the Pope, who ordered him to make peace with Becket. Henry met the archbishop, but refused to give Becket the 'kiss of peace' – the traditional sign of regal forgiveness. Nevertheless, Becket decided that he could return to England, only to cause fury far and wide by promptly excommunicating the Archbishop of York and the Bishops of London and Salisbury. Was this another act in yet another failed attempt to extort something from the king? Whatever it was, the reaction was swift. Leaving Canterbury for Winchester via London, the archbishop set off to meet the young king. Although he was met by cheering crowds as he entered the capital, he was also faced with a group of knights, who told him that not only was he not to meet the Young King Henry, he was to return to Canterbury forthwith and remain there. On his return, Becket learned of more bad news: Ranulf de Broc, whom he had excommunicated four years earlier and was living in the archbishop's castle at Saltwood, had captured his ships and stolen the wine they carried. Not only that, de Broc had sent for all his men-at-arms and was intent on surrounding the cathedral, either to arrest Becket if he tried to ignore the king's command that he remain in Canterbury, or simply to keep him there. On Christmas Eve, de Broc's nephew, Robert, guarding one of the roads into the city, came across one of the archbishop's pack horses, cut its tail off and paraded it in front of an irate Becket. That night, Robert's name was added to the list of those who were now excommunicated.

But far worse than occupied property, blockading soldiers or mutilated animals was about to befall the archbishop. Four knights – with or without the king's knowledge – were on their way from Normandy to bring the matter to an end.

Much is made of a supposed remark made by the king, in which he asked if no one could get rid of 'this troublesome priest'. In fact, Henry had already put into action a plan entirely of his own making. The king had decided to present Becket with an ultimatum: either he had to fall into line with Henry's demands or he would be arrested and tried on charges – probably of treason. The king's party was led by William de Mandeville, the Earl of Essex, a trusted and loyal counsellor. He was accompanied by Saher de Quincy, who held the lordship of Bourne in Cambridgeshire, and Richard de Humet, the king's constable. The party appeared to be in no hurry and, after splitting up, only de Humet arrived at Southampton to meet the young king, based at Winchester. On his arrival, de Humet ordered the royal bodyguards to take a group of knights to Canterbury and arrest the archbishop, whilst Essex and de Quincy would keep watch on the coast in case Becket attempted another flight to France. It was a cumbersome and drawn-out plan that would not only give Henry the cover he needed for any subsequent enquiry into the events which might follow, but would allow time for his real plan to take effect. And if his real aim failed to achieve the intended outcome, there was always the possibility – indeed, probability – that the final outcome, instigated by de Quincy, would be the same.

As the Earl of Essex's plodding mission set about its business, another group of four English knights arrived at Saltwood Castle and spent the evening plotting with Ranulf de Broc.

Their probable leader, Reginald FitzUrse, carried a shield which bore the image of an aggressive bear in recognition of his surname (meaning 'Son of a bear'). He was married and owned lands in Somerset, Northamptonshire, Montgomery and Kent. Although he could claim a connection with the royal family – his mother was said to have been an illegitimate daughter of Henry I – he had gained his position at court by an introduction from Thomas Becket.

William de Tracy not only had a mother who was another illegitimate child of Henry I, but also had an ancestor who was the sister of King Edward the Confessor. Married and with a son, de Tracy owned the lordship of the manors of Toddington in Gloucestershire and Moretonhampstead in Devon. The latter county also provided him with lands as the Baron of Bradnich.

The highest ranking of the four was Hugh de Morville, Lord of Westmorland. Unmarried, de Morville had been in the king's service since 1158. He was the owner of Knaresborough Castle in Yorkshire.

Richard le Bret was the most junior of the four knights, both in age and rank. He was without property as his father was only a tenant of a Somerset landlord. He must have had some qualities, however, which had seen him knighted and in the king's service – possibly an association with William, the king's brother.

Saltwood Castle in the mid-nineteenth century.

Of the four knights, three – FitzUrse, de Tracy and de Morville – had paid homage to Becket when, as chancellor, he had been given the responsibility of looking after the raising of Henry, the king's son. It is also possible that all four owed a higher loyalty than to Becket or even the king – they may have been confreres of the Knights Templar.

During their deliberations at Saltwood Castle, Ranulf de Broc called out the garrisons at Dover, Bletchingley Castle and Rochester. He intended to surround the cathedral at Canterbury to prevent the archbishop's escape.

The next day, 29 December 1170, the four knights, leaving an escort of other knights at the gate of the cathedral, removed their weapons and entered the archbishop's palace. There they found Becket in an inner chamber talking to a monk. Ignored by the archbishop, the knights sat down on the floor and waited until Becket acknowledged their presence. When he eventually did so, FitzUrse immediately demanded in the name of the king that the archbishop go to Winchester to make his peace with the Young King. Not unnaturally, Becket forcibly reminded the knights that he had tried to make such a visit, but had been prevented from doing so. FitzUrse then switched to the excommunication of the Archbishop of York and other bishops. It did not take long for the knights to become tired of what looked to be a most likely interminable discourse on who was right and who was wrong. Voices became raised and the archbishop stood up as he began to issue threats against all who opposed him. Monks and clerks, listening in an outside chamber, rushed in alarmed at the commotion. FitzUrse ordered the room to be cleared, but no one moved. Thwarted in a possible attempt to arrest the archbishop, FitzUrse gave the order that the archbishop was not to be allowed to leave the cathedral. He then left the room with the other knights, as Becket shouted abuse at their retreating backs.

Becket rages at the knights.

At about 4.15 p.m., with daylight fading, the four knights returned to their weapons and armed themselves with their swords as knights and soldiers burst on to the cathedral grounds shouting 'King's men!' The commotion caused the monks inside the great hall of the palace to slam shut the heavy door, leaving FitzUrse and the other knights outside banging ineffectually against its solid woodwork. At this, Robert de Broc broke a window and let himself in, rushing to the door to admit the four knights and a sword-carrying sub-deacon, Hugh of Horsea. Climbing the staircase from the palace to the cloisters, they entered the great church by the door of the north transept. There they saw Becket as he stood on the steps leading from the north aisle to the choir. The archbishop turned and descended back down the steps accompanied by a small group of monks. Standing at the entrance to the transept, with the altar of St Benedict behind him, Becket faced the knights who bore down on him with shouts of 'Traitor!'

Turning aside the accusation, Becket replied, 'What do you want?' FitzUrse, casting aside the axe he was carrying, grabbed Becket by his cloak with a view to dragging him off under arrest. Whilst the other monks fled in terror, one, Edward Grim, remained and held on to the archbishop in an undignified scuffle. De Tracy then joined in the attempt to haul away the archbishop as de Morville turned and faced a gathering crowd of townspeople, who had entered the cathedral for the evening service.

In blind frustration at the fact that his great mission had been reduced to an unseemly public tug of war, FitzUrse raised his sword and brought it down hard upon Becket's head. The blade sliced into the archbishop's skull and cut Grim's arm to the bone. At this, the monk fell back clutching his almost severed arm, and the archbishop reeled and collapsed in a fountain of blood. As he fell, de Tracy then hacked once more at Becket's head. Finally, with the archbishop sprawled upon the stone flags of the transept, le Bret stepped forward. 'Take this for the love of my lord William, the king's brother', he shouted, and brought his sword down with such force that it sliced off the top of Becket's skull before breaking against the stone floor. As if to underline the horror of the event, the sub-deacon, Hugh of Horsea, took his sword and pushed it into the archbishop's skull, scattering Becket's brains over the floor. 'Let us be away, knights,' he said, in an almost matter-of-fact manner. 'This fellow will not get up again.'

Astonishingly, the death of Thomas Becket was not followed by a huge outpouring of public grief. Many, who remembered his time as the chancellor, merely felt that he had received his due reward. The Pope mourned for a week and then got on with his business, which included punishing King Henry by making him pay for the services of 200 Knights Templar at Jerusalem for one year and demanding that he went on Crusade for three years, unless excused by the Pope himself. Time spent fighting the Saracens in Spain was to count in his favour. There were a few other penalties such as the restoration of church property. Henry himself underwent a pantomime public chastisement which verged on being little more than a public relations stunt. Much further action against the king was avoided when he took on an invasion of Ireland – whilst doing the Pope's work in that country he could hardly be re-directed to disabling penances on account of a dead archbishop. There was also a question arising from the very practices that Becket firmly supported: if a cleric who murdered a layman could not be tried in a secular court, how could a layman who murdered a cleric be tried in an ecclesiastical court? Few, if any, cared. Just two years after Becket's death, Henry agreed to abolish most of the laws he had brought against the Church in England, including those bringing clergy before a secular court and those forbidding an appeal to Rome without royal consent. His reason for bringing in the laws in the first place was safely in his grave.

Most surprising of all was the fact that there had been no hue-and-cry against the four knights who had carried out the brutal murder. They had made their way to de Morville's castle at Knaresborough in Yorkshire where they stayed for about a year. Whilst there, they paid for and supervised the building (or possible completion) of the church at Alkborough in Lincolnshire. This information was recorded on a plaque in the church chancel until it was removed in 1690.

Clearly the church tower at Alkborough was built before the knights took an interest. It is late Saxon in design, with its sides pierced by narrow windows with rounded tops typical of the period. However, the tower was later adorned with additional windows, this time of the Early English 'lancet' pattern, once again narrow, but with a pointed arch at the top. This style of architecture appears to have just one source – but it is very difficult to prove.

During their time in the Holy Land, the Knights Templar built several castles, employing their own masons ('mason brothers') to carry out the work. It was inevitable that these masons would have enquired into the building methods of the Muslims, in particular the use of pointed arches. This style of building gave greater strength to the structure, allowed wider windows and, consequently, let more light into the building. It is not difficult to imagine Templar masons, and possibly Templar wealth, being involved with the building of the great cathedrals that sprang up all over western Europe when the Templars were at the height of their power. In the church of St John the Baptist (a favourite saint's name for Templar churches) at Alkborough, the addition of lancet windows to the Saxon tower clearly indicates an eastern influence. Such a design could suggest that the church at Alkborough is one of the very earliest churches in England (possibly in western Europe) to be built in what later became known in England as the Early English and, later still, the Gothic style.

Within easy walking distance from the church, Alkborough has another surprise. Cut into the turf of an open area, overlooking the confluence of the rivers Ouse and Trent where they form the River Humber, is a 43ft maze. It is very similar to one at Chartres Cathedral – another building that was built less than twenty years after the Alkborough church, using the Gothic style of architecture. Suggestions as to the origins of the Alkborough maze run from the Romans to the Tudors, but most experts seem to agree on a medieval origin.

The maze is known as 'Julian's Bower', a name which gives more than one possible link with the four knights who murdered Becket. The weakest of these lies in a record of 1697, when it was described as 'Gillian's Bore'. 'Gillian' could just be a corruption of the French version of 'William' – 'Guillaume'. One of the knights was William de Tracy. On the other hand,

such mazes were often known as 'Solomon's Labyrinth' or
'Chemin de Jerusalem' – both with obvious connections to
the Knights Templar. The best clue, however, comes when
the 'Bore' of the 1697 description is retained in place of the
'Bower' (a shaded, leafy area, which does not fit the site at
all). It then becomes 'Julian's Bore'. St Julian was the patron
saint and protector of pilgrims and travellers – the spiritual
equivalent of the early Knights Templar. As for 'Bore', in its
earliest usage it meant 'to make weary by being repetitive, dull,
and tedious' – the continuous walking (possibly on the knees)
making a perfect medieval form of penance.

Further connections with the Knights Templar became
clear when the Pope sent the four knights to serve in the
Holy Land for fourteen years 'in knightly arms in the
Temple'. Before leaving England, de Tracy gave half his land
to the Knights Templar. Legend has them dying whilst on
such service and being buried in the grounds of the Temple
at Jerusalem. However, there is good evidence that they
returned to England. At Mortehoe church in the north of
Devon there is the tomb of a Sir William de Tracy. Opinion
is divided as to whether or not this is the actual murderer
of Becket, or a later priest with the same name who died in
1322. The latter suggestion is based upon mention of a donation by the similarly named 'one-time Rector of Mortehoe'
to Exeter Cathedral of 20s in 1323. The image on the top of
the Purbeck marble tomb slab certainly appears to be dressed
as a priest (which does not exclude the Becket knight). On
the side of the tomb are images of St Catherine and St Mary
Magdalene – an image of St Catherine can be found among
the Templar carvings at Royston, Hertfordshire. There is also
the three lions coat of arms of Richard I and two other heraldic arms on the tomb. In some quarters, it is thought that
these tomb decorations are nothing more than the recycling
of images from another part of the church, such as the reredos

of an altar. Carved onto the top slab is an almost lost Norman-French inscription which can be read as '*Syree Williame de Trace – Il enat eeys-Meercy*' (or, '*Syre lame de Trace – alme eyt mercy*'), which may be translated as 'Sir William de Tracy – He is at ease – Thank you' or as 'Sir William de Tracy – The Lord have mercy on his soul'. There are two problems for the supporters of the theory that the tomb is of a fourteenth-century priest. Firstly, the inscription is not in Latin – the language used on the tombs of medieval priests – and secondly, according to church historians, priests in the Middle Ages were buried with their feet to the west (presumably so that, when they rise from the tomb at the second coming, they will face their congregations). The figure on the tomb at Mortehoe church has its feet to the east, the custom for lay persons, including knights.

Alkborough church with its lower Saxon and later Early English (Gothic) windows.

Above left: The labyrinth at Alkborough known as 'Julian's Bower'.

Above right: The chalice on the chest of the image of William de Tracy. (Courtesy of the Reverend G. King-Smith)

However, of considerably greater significance is the fact that displayed on the chest of the occupant's tomb-top figure is the image of a chalice. The cup is held up to the viewer solely by the tips of the fingers of each hand as if it was a delicate and precious trophy. Long assumed to be a chalice associated with the Holy Communion, the vessel, in fact, is missing the key feature which, throughout the Middle Ages, was always used to indicate that it was intended for use at the Sacrament. The host is nowhere to be seen, which is usually shown as a disc either hovering above the chalice, or emerging halfway above the vessel's lip. Nor is there any other paraphernalia associated with the Eucharist, such as the paten or the protective cloth. It is nothing more than a plain, unadorned chalice of the type that Becket was desperate to possess.

As for Becket, it was not long before a cascade of miracles took place before his tomb and he was canonised just three years after his death. In addition to a spectacular shrine built to house his bones in Canterbury Cathedral, relics of the saint were put in beautifully decorated gold and enamel reliquaries showing the death of the archbishop. In the scene (copied many times elsewhere) he is being attacked before an altar on which is a golden (gilded?) cup. This object is clearly not a chalice intended for Holy Communion as, again, it is not accompanied by a paten, protective cloth or any of the other paraphernalia or symbols of the Sacrament. It stands alone as if in silent remembrance of Becket's attempt to obtain the holy relic against the wishes of the king and against the might of the Templars.

Then, as if fate had not been harsh enough with the covetous prelate, his and his fellow clerics' greed for relics revisited him, even after death. A Christchurch monk named Benedict was appointed Abbot of Peterborough Abbey in 1176. Finding his abbey short of notable relics, Benedict visited Canterbury and took away (i.e. stole) two of the flagstones on which Becket had been murdered, along with two vases of the martyr's blood and pieces of Becket's clothing. With the flagstones, the abbot built an altar on which to display his newly acquired relics.

Even more bizarrely, a Brother Roger, who had been appointed as 'Keeper of the Altars of the Martyrdom' at Canterbury Cathedral, was offered no less than the post of abbot of the nearby Augustinian abbey if he stole part of Becket's skull and handed it over to the neighbouring Augustinians. Not only did Brother Roger eagerly comply with the request, but the new owners of the relic boasted widely of their successful initiative and enterprise – such was the blatant zeal in the world of clerics for highly prized relics. Becket, it seems, was not different, just better connected.

Even then, the story of the archbishop and the relics is not quite finished. High above the shrine built for the saint, a crescent moon, curving towards the east, was fixed to the arched ceiling. The reason why this particular form of decoration was used was never made clear. It has been suggested that this Islamic symbol represents an old rumour that Becket's mother was a Muslim, which has never been justified or confirmed. Another suggestion is that it is representative of the time when

Becket – as St Thomas – was the patron saint of a hospital in Acre, and it was claimed that his spiritual support helped drive the Saracens from the city walls. It has also been suggested that the crescent is simply a Crusader souvenir, although why it was chosen to be sited above Becket's shrine is not made clear. One idea removes the link with Islam entirely. As the position of the shrine approximates to the normal location of a cathedral's 'Lady Chapel', it has been proposed that the crescent represents Mary, the mother of Christ, who is frequently seen in the presence of – and even standing on – a crescent moon (from Revelations 12:1 'and the moon under her feet').

When, in the early part of the nineteenth century, the crescent was taken down to be re-gilded, it was found to be made of ironwood (*Parrotia Persica*), which, at the time of the Crusades, was found only in the Middle East. Of greater note is a contemporary comment: 'It [the crescent] had been fastened to the groining by a large nail of very singular shape, with a large square head, apparently of foreign manufacture.' Could it be possible that one of the greatest relics in Christianity, one of the nails used in Christ's Crucifixion, was used to nail the symbol of Islam to the roof of the cathedral immediately above the shrine to St Thomas Becket? If so, why?

The crescent above the site of Becket's shrine.

6

THE ARTHURIAN DAWN

If Henry had rid himself of one thorn in his side, there were plenty more to annoy him. With Eleanor in Aquitaine, Henry turned to the problems of his sons. John, still a child, was given the castles at Loudon, Mirebeau and Chinon. All the castles were in Anjou, a county that had been promised to the young Henry. This angered the Young King, who demanded to rule in his own right England, Anjou or Normandy. When this was refused he fled to France and sought the aid of Louis VII. There he was joined by his brothers Richard and Geoffrey. It did not take long for a full-scale revolt against Henry to break out, probably engineered, in part, by Eleanor. Henry reacted in fury, driving back his enemies until Eleanor decided to flee and join her eldest sons. In late September 1173, dressed as a knight, she rode from Poitiers with just a small escort and ran straight into some of her own knights who were supporters of Henry. Delivered to the king, Eleanor was kept under guard whilst Henry went to Poitiers and destroyed the court his queen had established. The king then crossed over to England in July 1174 and sent Eleanor to be confined within the walls of Salisbury (Old Sarum) Castle. She was to remain there for the best part of fifteen years.

During her time at Poitiers, Eleanor had created a court noted for its elegance, style, culture and the elevation of women into almost objects of worship. For Eleanor and her 'Ladies Court', men – especially knights – should be bound to a single sentiment: chivalry.

Previously, with few exceptions, knighthood was meant for little more than warfare. A totally brutish business, a knight was expected to give no quarter or mercy, but to get on with the business of destroying his liege's enemies. If women or children got in the way, then they had to be cleared away with the same ruthlessness as the men. In fact, the men were more likely to survive as, if they were also knights, their horse and armour could be taken and the knights themselves held for ransom. Weakness in anyone, friend or foe, was something to be exploited, which included taking advantage of defenceless women.

There had been exceptions. In May 1168 Eleanor had been out riding with a small escort, including the Earl of Salisbury, when they were ambushed by Guy de Lusignan, one of the queen's own vassals, who had the intention of capturing Eleanor and the earl and holding them to ransom. Eleanor bolted for the safety of her castle as the earl was killed and the escort scattered. Only one knight stood his ground – 22-year-old William FitzJohn, the son of the same John FitzGilbert, Marshal of England, who had been part of the plot to draw Becket to Northampton before the archbishop's flight from the country. The young knight drew his sword and charged straight at the ambushers. It was later recorded that he fought like 'a wild boar attacked by hounds' before being brought down and captured. When she heard of FitzJohn's conduct, Eleanor paid the ransom and, on his release, presented him with horses, rich garments and gold. Taken into the royal service, as Eleanor was put behind the walls of Salisbury Castle, FitzJohn was appointed the guardian and teacher of the Young King Henry.

Eleanor and her court had decided to change the role of the knight. The example of the Knights Templar had shown that knights could exercise discipline and be bound by rules of conduct, with no loss of courage or martial vigour. William FitzJohn had shown the matchless courage required of a knight in defence of a lady. Instead of following the old practice of trampling on the feeble, her knights were to be expected to show mercy to the weak and defenceless, yet to be a scourge of the evil-doer. They should replace pride with humility and be prepared to sacrifice themselves in a good cause. They should fear only God and face overwhelming odds with clear courage. They must be honourable and behave with exemplary conduct. They must be eternally faithful and treat all women, regardless of age, rank or condition, with the utmost courtesy.

What the knights themselves actually thought of this is not known, but the seeds of chivalry were certainly sown and were soon to take root in a most unexpected quarter.

Among the regular visitors at Eleanor's court was her eldest daughter by Louis VII – Marie, Countess of Champagne. Much taken with the idea of the noble knight, Marie, with the support of her mother, acted as patron for Chrétien de Troyes, a poet who, whilst at the court, had written the story of *Erec and Enide*, a tale of one of King Arthur's knights who struggled with the competing interests of his marriage and his duty to the king. With the breaking up of Eleanor's court by Henry, de Troyes eventually entered the service of Phillip, Count of Flanders, an unsuccessful suitor of Marie of Champagne, who not only supported him during the writing of his unfinished tale *Percival, the Story of the Grail*, but also provided him with the theme from an earlier version. By the time it was finished, around 1190, King Henry II was dead, the Young King was dead, Eleanor had been released from her prison and her son, Richard, was King of England.

The story of King Arthur found its roots in three different strands. The oldest was to be found in the Saxon invasion of Britain in AD 450. Over the next sixty-five years the indigenous Celts were driven back into Cornwall and Wales. Then, around AD 515, after decades of settlement, an advance party of Saxons came up against a much larger, or more experienced, Celtic army – probably at Liddington Hill, near the Wiltshire town of Swindon. The Saxons, with many of their warriors now settled as farmers, were wiped out, guilty of over-extending their lines of communication. For the Saxons, such a defeat would have presented little cause for concern – indeed, it might have been welcomed. The time had probably come for a consolidation of their gains as there would have been little risk of a full-scale Celtic counter-attack. To deal with the problem of defeat, they only had to look to their gods. Woden, the chief god, was known to be capricious. If he decided to throw his mighty spear at the Saxons' enemies, then the Saxons could not lose and the 'war fetters' would fall upon the foe. If, on the other hand, Woden decided that he would fight against the Saxons, they could not win, and would accept their fate without complaint.

Once this version of events reached the Celts, they took to their hearts their previously unrecognised ally who had fought alongside them as a great spiritual warrior. Before long, colourfully embroidered tales of this new hero were being recounted by the bards around the campfires and hearths of the Britons.

The second strand of the story of King Arthur starts with the arrival of Christianity at the end of the sixth century. The Saxon gods found themselves under attack in the east of England, whilst in the west, the Celts felt the pressure of Irish monks trying to convert them to the new religion. The Irish knew that the best way to obtain converts was to find common ground between the conflicting religions. Once they had converted their fellow Celts they came up against the Saxon deities. There they found the link they were looking for in the way that Christians referred to their God – as 'Father'. The Saxon god Woden was known by several names.

One, for example, was 'Grim', which gave rise to geographical names as varied as 'Grimsby', 'Grimes Dic' (Grimsdyke) and 'Grimes Graves'. One of the most popular names, however, whether the chief Norse god appeared as Woden, Wuotan, Wodan, Voden or Odin, was 'Alfdr' – 'Allfather'. By gradually associating 'Father' with 'Allfather', it was hoped that the Saxons would be more easily converted, almost by subterfuge. But an extraordinary thing happened. The Irish 'Father' began to take on the attributes of Woden. And the Irish word for 'Father' was 'Athir'.

The third strand came with the arrival of the Vikings, bringing with them their version of the same gods as the Saxons. The newcomers soon found a home for their old gods as their leaders found it more convenient to accept Christianity. Odin, Thor, Tyr, Baldur and others blended in with the Saxons' Woden, Thunor, Tiw and Frig.

With the three strands now interwoven, but still under pressure from the Christian Church, which would not have favoured the old gods still being in existence, someone – almost certainly amongst the Celts – reached into the essence of the pagan pantheon and produced a new legend based on mighty but fallible warriors, their leader ready to return when his people faced danger.

One important early source of the new legend was the Welsh prose romance *Culhwch and Olwen*, which built upon even earlier references. The leader was Arthur (from 'Athir'), a noble, kingly warrior, yet full of human flaws. Then came Cai, a warrior of strength and endurance; anything that was held in his hand remained dry despite the hardest rain, and so great was the heat from his body that his comrades could use him to light fires. Thunor (the Saxon version of the Viking 'Thor') was the god of rain. He was also so hot that sparks flew from his beard, and he alone of all the gods was forbidden to cross the Bifrost (rainbow) Bridge for fear his heat would destroy it.

In place of Thor's pagan hammer, Cai used a sword, a wound from which no healer could mend. The influence on the transformation was not entirely Celtic. The Saxon 'Lacnunga' – a collection of spells and herbal remedies – had a spell 'Against the Toothache' which can only partly be translated:

> Sing this against the toothache, when the sun is set, very often:
> Caio laio quaque ofer saeloficia, the man slew the worm.
> Here name the man and his father, then say:
> Lilumenne it aches most when it mitigates,
> It cools most when it burns hottest on earth. Fintamen.

According to Norse mythology it was Thor who slew the Midgard Worm. The last line of the spell pleads for the presence of great heat to 'cool' the sufferer's pain. To the Celts he had become Cai, to the Saxons, Caio. To later generations he became the Arthurian knight – Sir Kay.

Next came the formidable warrior 'Bedwyr' who, despite being one-handed, could shed blood on a battlefield faster than the others. He was armed with a spear that made one wound on entering his enemy's body, but made nine when it was withdrawn. Tyr, the Viking god of war and courage, was the only god brave enough to act as hostage by placing his hand between the jaws of the giant wolf Fenrir (or 'Fenris') whilst the other gods bound the monster with unbreakable bonds. When Fenrir realised he could not escape from the bonds, he bit off Tyr's hand. Again, a Saxon involvement may be found in the Anglo-Saxon word for war and battle – 'beado' or 'beadu'. Thus, the Arthurian knight Sir Bedivere came into being.

Gawain, the 'perfect knight' of early Arthurian legend, is found in *Culhwch and Olwen* as 'Gwalchmei', a much-beloved, golden-haired nephew of Arthur whose strength mysteriously increased towards midday and thereafter gradually faded.

Odin had a son named Baldur who, with the exception of the mistletoe, nothing in the worlds of gods or men would harm, such was the universal love of all things for him. He was worshipped as a sun god.

Another nephew of Arthur in *Culhwch and Olwen* was Medrault, the evil knight who fought on the side of the Saxons. In the Norse myths, Loki, blood-brother to Odin and father of the wolf Fenrir and other monsters, turned traitor and fought against the gods at Ragnarok, the terrible, final battle between good and evil. Medrault was later to appear in the Arthurian legends as the malevolent Sir Mordred.

Arthur's queen also makes an appearance as 'Gwenhwyvar'. The origin of this name is unknown, but the first element – 'gwen' – means 'white' in the Celtic language. Woden's wife, Frig, dressed in robes of purest white, and in parts of Germany she was known as 'The White Lady'. In the stories of both Guinevere (as she was to become) and Frig, there is more than a suggestion of marital misconduct. Both were the daughters of giants.

At Ragnarok, the great battle between the gods and their enemies, the giant snake that encircles the Earth, the Midgard Worm, slithers on to the land to join the conflict. Loki's offspring, the wolf Fenrir, rushes onto the field of battle with its jaws open until they reach from the earth to the sky. They are joined by a host of frost and fire giants. At this, the god Heimdall alerts the gods with a blast on his giant horn and the doors of Valhalla are flung open for the gods and heroes to storm over the rainbow bridge to pour onto the field of battle. Thor kills the Midgard Worm instantly but is sprayed with poison and dies. Tyr faces Garm, the dread hound of the Underworld, and is crushed to death between its jaws – but not until he has brought about its own death by thrusting his sword down the monster's throat. Odin is overwhelmed by the wolf Fenrir, but one of the chief god's sons, Vidar, grabs the wolf by the gaping jaws and tears him apart. Heimdall, also a son of Odin, kills Loki. At the end of the day, only the fire giant Surt remains alive, though maddened by the rage of battle. He stumbles over the Earth spreading fire that ensures the end of mankind.

The Arthurian legend ends with the battle of Camlann – a Celtic word meaning 'ferocious battle'. In some versions, the battle is started when a knight draws his sword to defend himself against a snake. In the ensuing clash, Arthur and Mordred come face to face and kill each other. Arthur's body is taken to the waters by Sir Bedivere, where it is placed upon a boat escorted by three queens – women probably representing Urd, Verdandi and Skuld, the three Fates of Norse mythology.

Such was the framework upon which Chrétien de Troyes hung his works. He introduced Lancelot, Percival, the Lance and the Grail, which in de Troyes' works was neither 'Holy' nor a chalice, but a serving dish containing a sacramental host. Introduced as 'un graal', it was clearly never meant to be important to the story in its own right, but existed as little more than a prop. Interwoven with Percival's search for the Grail (during which Percival is expected to ask an important question), is the story of Gawain who is searching for the Lance with which Jesus was pierced whilst on the Cross. The Lance, from which blood perpetually bleeds from its tip, continued, in de Troyes' work, with its association with the Grail – even though the Grail is not represented as the vessel which was used to catch Christ's blood.

No one has been able to definitely ascertain why, but de Troyes failed to complete his poem. It may have been nothing more complicated than his death, but, whatever the cause, four 'continuations' took up the story, each providing a different conclusion. The second continuation introduced the concept of the Christian Grail – the vessel used to contain Christ's blood. The third identifies the Lance as being that of a Roman soldier named Longinus.

Ragnarok. Thor forces the Midgard Worm's jaws open with his shield as he raises his hammer. Odin is about to thrust his spear down the throat of the Fenrir wolf as a Valhalla hero struggles with a fire giant. Behind them, more heroes pour across the rainbow Bifrost Bridge.

Then a most surprising thing happened. After a fire in 1184, which destroyed an ancient wattle church at Glastonbury, the graves of King Arthur and his queen were discovered close by. This proved to be a most fortuitous find, especially for the monarchy who could, at last, now rest assured that Arthur would not rise again and challenge the Crown of England. Furthermore, following the example of the martyrdom of Becket at Canterbury, the site would attract pilgrims, which in turn meant money. So much wealth arrived at Glastonbury that before long, a magnificent abbey had been built on the site of the old church.

It has been suggested that the 'find' was nothing more than a clerical confidence trick aimed to raise funds for a replacement building, but excavations have shown that a grave did actually exist there. On the other hand, the discovery of a grave in a graveyard is hardly remarkable.

Sometime around 1200, a new version of the story emerged, one that not only was quite different from what had gone before, but one that rewrote history. Robert de Boron was a Burgundian poet in the service of Gautier de Montbéliard, Lord of Montfaucon. Like de Troyes before him, de Boron was given a guide by his patron either in the form of an already existing book or by a written instruction on the direction the story was to take.

For de Boron, the Grail had become the chalice which was used by Christ at the Last Supper and then by Joseph of Arimathea to collect Christ's blood after He had been pierced by the Lance. Joseph of Arimathea brought the (now 'Holy') Grail to France from where it was taken to England by his brother-in-law, Bron. This is a curious twist brought about, perhaps, by deliberate policy. De Boron's patron, de Montbéliard, may have already known the de Lusignan family (who had killed the Earl of Salisbury in their attempt to capture Eleanor, Queen of England). De Montbéliard eventually married Bourgogne de Lusignan, daughter of King Amaury of Jerusalem, and was to become Regent of Cyprus during the minority of his brother-in-law, Hugh de Lusignan (Hugh I), nephew of Guy and son of Amaury – both of whom had been involved in the ambush of Eleanor, and had been exiled as a result. Assuming they knew of it, the de Lusignans would be more than happy to see Eleanor's role in the gaining of the chalice obliterated. It is also likely that de Montbéliard would have had a close connection with the Knights Templar. Now that the relic was firmly in their hands, they also might have been pleased with any suggestion that both confirmed its provenance and provided a 'historical' route to its origins; especially as de Boron places the final resting place of the Holy Grail in the Vale of Avalon, on the White Island – England.

Almost 300 years later, Sir Thomas Malory's *Le Morte d'Arthur* retained the link with the Knights Templar. When Sir Galahad found himself without a shield he arrived at a white abbey where a monk took him to an altar 'where hung a snow-white shield bearing in its midst a red cross'. The monk then told the knight that 'none but the worthiest of knights may bear this shield'. Galahad's companion, Sir Bagdemagus, then decides to test the shield's powers and rides to a hermitage in a 'fair valley'. There he is met and charged by a knight in white armour riding a white horse. Bagdemagus is unseated and the white knight hands the shield to a squire with the instructions to return it to Galahad: 'for this shield shall not be borne but by him that hath no living peer.'

There were to be several further variations of the story of King Arthur, his knights and the Holy Grail. But one almost forgotten early thirteenth-century account stands out from the rest. *Perlesvaus* or *The High History of the Holy Graal* is an anonymous work which is fictitiously attributed to 'Josephus', who 'set it in remembrance by the annunciation of the voice of an angel'. In this account, Joseph of Arimathea:

Sir Galahad bearing the white shield with the red cross.

> honoured the body [of Christ] the most he might, rather laid it along
> in the Holy Sepulchre and kept safe the lance whereof He was smit-
> ten in the side and the most Holy Vessel wherein they that believed
> on Him received with awe the blood that ran down from His wounds
> when He was set upon the rood.

At this stage, the Holy Grail (accompanied by the Spear or Lance) still remains merely a receptacle for liquid – holy or otherwise.

Early in the story, three women enter Arthur's court, one of them bearing a shield with a red cross. The leader of the women tells Arthur:

> The shield that this damsel beareth belonged to Joseph, the good
> soldier knight that took down Our Lord of hanging on the rood.
> I make you a present thereof in such wise as I shall tell you, to wit,
> that you keep the shield for a knight that shall come hither for the
> same, and you shall make it hang on this column in the midst of
> your hall, and guard it in such wise as that none may take it and
> hang at his neck save he only. And of this shield shall he achieve the
> Graal, and another shield shall he leave here in the hall, red, with a
> white hart.

Later, Sir Gawain learns from a priest of the shield left hanging in the hall:

> The shield whereon was the red cross, that she left at the court of
> King Arthur, signifieth the most holy shield of the rood that never
> none durst lift save God alone.

Eventually, the shield is collected by the pure knight, Sir Percival, who demonstrates his purity (whilst carrying a different shield) when he encounters a damsel in distress. So pleased is she to see him that:

She goeth to meet him, and holdeth his stirrup and would have kissed his foot, but he avoideth it and crieth to her. 'Ill do you herein, damsel!' And therewith she melteth in tears of weeping and prayeth him right sweetly.

Sir Percival also encounters a pagan queen who tells him of a dream she had of the Crucifixion:

And another folk were there that collected His blood in a most Holy Vessel that one of them held for it.

Later, he learns how the cross on the shield came about. Two men bow before him and kiss the shield whilst telling him that, originally, Joseph of Arimathea had a white shield:

but no cross was there on the shield before the death of Jesus Christ. But he had it set thereon after the Crucifixion of Jesus Christ for the sake of the Saviour he loved so well.

In the meantime, Sir Gawain reaches the castle of the Fisher King, a king whose wounds will not heal until a pure knight asks of whom it does serve. After meeting the king, and being reminded of the need to ask the question, Gawain goes to dine in the great hall. As he sits at the table with the other knights:

Thereon, lo you, two damsels that issue forth of a chapel, whereof the one holdeth in her hands the most Holy Graal, and the other the Lance whereof the point bleedeth thereinto. And the one goeth beside the other in the midst of the hall where the knights and Messire Gawain sat at meat, and so sweet a smell and so holy came to them therefrom that they forgot to eat. Messire Gawain looketh at the Graal, and it seemeth to him that a chalice was therein, albeit none was there at this time, and he seeth the point of the Lance whence the red blood ran thereinto, and it seemeth to him that he seeth two angels that bear two candlesticks of gold filled with candles. And the damsels pass before Messire Gawain, and go into another chapel. And Messire Gawain is thoughtful, and so great a joy cometh to him that naught remembereth he in his thinking save of God only. The knights are all daunted and sorrowful in their hearts, and look at Messire Gawain. Thereupon behold you the damsels that issue forth of the chamber and come again before Messire Gawain, and him seemeth that he seeth three there where before he had seen but two, and seemeth him that in the midst of the Graal he seeth the figure of a child. The Master of the Knights beckoneth to Messire Gawain. Messire Gawain looketh before him and seeth three drops of blood fall upon the table. He was all abashed to look at them and spoke no word.

Therewith the damsels pass forth and the knights are all adread and look one at the other. Howbeit Messire Gawain may not withdraw his eyes from the three drops of blood, and when he would fain kiss them they vanish away, whereof he is right sorrowful, for he may not set his hand nor aught that of him is to touch thereof. Therewithal behold you the two damsels that come again before the table and seemeth to Messire Gawain that there are three, and he looketh up and it seemeth him to be the Graal all in flesh, and he seeth above as him thinketh, a King crowned, nailed upon a rood, and the spear was still fast in His side. Messire Gawain seeth it and hath great pity thereof, and of nought doth he remember him save of the pain that this King suffereth. And the Master of the Knights summoneth him again by word of mouth, and telleth him that if he delayeth longer, never more will he recover it. Messire Gawain is silent, as he that heareth not the knight speak, and looketh upward. But the damsels go back into the chapel and carry back the most Holy Graal and the Lance, and the knights make the tablecloths be taken away and rise from meat and go into another hall and leave Messire Gawain all alone.

Because of some impure act in his past, Sir Gawain cannot see the Grail and the Spear, and does not ask the question. As if in compensation, he goes on to win a great relic – the sword with which John the Baptist was beheaded.

Sir Percival, however, arrives at a castle on an island where he is invited into the great hall. There:

> One of the Masters clappeth his hands thrice, and three and thirty men came into the hall all of a company. They were clad in white garments, and not one of them but had a red cross in the midst of his breast.

Eventually, Sir Percival achieves the Grail, not by asking the question, but by force of arms. At Castle Mortal, wherein lay the Chapel of the Grail, Sir Percival faces nine bridges, each guarded by three knights. The castle is also guarded by two lions, one white and one red. Sir Percival learns that the white lion:

> is on God's side, and look at him whensoever your force shall fail you, and he will look at you likewise in such sort as that straightway you shall know his intent, by the will and pleasure of Our Saviour. Wherefore do according as you shall see that he would, for no intent will he have save good only, and to help you.

Another aid to Sir Percival is a white mule 'starred on the forehead with a red cross'. He is also to carry a banner, the design or colour of which is not portrayed as if such a description would be unnecessary.

Assisted by the white lion, the mule and the banner, and armed with sword, shield and lance, Sir Percival single-handedly takes the castle. Immediately:

> The Graal presented itself again in the chapel, and the lance whereof the point bleedeth, and the sword wherewith St. John was beheaded that Messire Gawain won, and the other holy relics whereof was right great plenty.

Eventually, in company with King Arthur and Sir Gawain, Sir Percival arrives at the Chapel of the Grail. There they see a procession of hermits carrying crosses and candles led by a man dressed in white. At the rear of the procession is a man carrying 'a bell with the clapper and all at his neck'. Such an item was unknown to the king and the knights.

> As soon as they [the hermits] came in to the holy chapel, they took the bell from the last and smote thereon at the altar, and then set it on the ground, and then began they the service, most holy and glorious. The history witnesseth us that in the land of King Arthur at this time there was not a single chalice. The Graal appeared at the sacring of the mass, in five several manners that none ought not to tell, for the secret things of the sacrament ought none to tell openly but he unto whom god hath given it. King Arthur beheld all the changes, the last whereof was the change into a chalice. And the hermit that chanted the mass found a brief under the corporal and declared the letters, to wit, that our Lord God would that in such vessel should his body be sacrificed, and that it should be set upon record. The history saith not that there were no chalices elsewhere, but that in all Great Britain and in the whole kingdom was none. King Arthur was right glad of this that he had seen, and had in remembrance the name and fashion of the most holy chalice.

Whilst God had told the king that such chalices were to be used throughout the kingdom, upon enquiry, Arthur learned that the bell was one of three made by King Solomon. One had been made for 'the Saviour of the World', the second 'for His sweet Mother' and the third for 'the honour of the Saints'. Now this third bell had also been brought 'hither by the commandment of God, who willeth that this should be the pattern of all those that shall be fashioned in the realm of this island where never aforetime have been none'.

Having achieved the Holy Grail, Sir Percival's last day in this world is announced when he 'came to the windows of the hall and saw the ship come with the white sail and the red cross thereon'.

Perlesvaus is written like a Knights Templar textbook. King Arthur, Sir Lancelot and Sir Gawain all provide examples of great courage and chivalry, but only one, Sir Percival, the knight of the red cross shield, achieves his aim by keeping to the Templar rules. Even a grateful attempt to kiss his foot by a damsel in distress is rejected almost with horror. The tale is set in the contemporary early thirteenth century and talks of 'the false law of the Sarrazins' (Saracens). The Castle Mortal, wherein is the Chapel of the Grail, is meant to represent Jerusalem and is in the hands of the Lord of the Moors – a name synonymous with 'Muslim' or 'Arab'. Sir Percival, in keeping with the Templar code of 'To the Enemies of Christ ferocious and inexorable', drowns the Lord of the Moors in the blood of his own knights. *Perlesvaus* settles the origins of the chalice and how it reached England. The white-clad, red cross knights are firmly established as the Keepers of the Grail and the chalice becomes the only type of vessel to be used at the Communion in England.

7

THE LIONHEART CRUSADE

The last years of King Henry's reign had not gone well. With Queen Eleanor under guard at Salisbury Castle, he may have thought the time had come when he could spend more time with his mistress, Rosamond Clifford. Instead, in 1174, he found himself fighting against his eldest son, the Young King Henry, who was being supported by Louis of France and Phillip of Flanders. Having beaten off his own heir and his allies, Henry asked Eleanor for a divorce, but the queen refused. Then, the following year, the fair Rosamond died and was buried in Godstow Abbey – only to later have her remains thrown out the building by Bishop Hugh of Lincoln.

In 1177 another attempt to get a divorce from Eleanor failed, and whilst Henry had his youngest son crowned King of Ireland, another son, Richard, was at perpetual war with the barons of Aquitaine. A botched attempt to appease the search for land from the Young King Henry and his brother Geoffrey, led to war between the two princes and their brother, Richard. In an effort to calm matters down, Henry went to Limoges in February 1183, only to come under attack from the Young King's bowmen on the city walls. Four months later, whilst on a rampage of vandalism in the Dordogne, the Young King looted the shrine at Rocamadour. Within hours he fell ill and, a week later, he was dead. Three years later, Prince Geoffrey died, leaving Henry with just two sons: the youngest and his favourite John, and Richard, Eleanor's favourite.

Then the darkest of news arrived from the Holy Land – not only had a Crusader army been destroyed, but Jerusalem had fallen to the infidels.

Saladin (from 'Salah ad-din Yussef') was of Kurdish background and had proved himself to be more than just another warrior. A skilful diplomat and strategist, Saladin preferred diplomacy and negotiation where possible, but where that failed, he believed equally in a military hammer-blow to achieve his aims. If necessary, he would personally execute any enemy who he felt behaved in a non-chivalrous, contemptible manner. By 1170, Saladin had manoeuvred himself into the position of Sultan of Egypt and consolidated his position until the ruler of Syria died. He then attacked Damascus and captured Syria. Other Muslim states fell to his forces until, in response to Crusader pressure that had even threatened Mecca, Saladin's army advanced into Galilee and clashed with a group of Knights Templar and Knights Hospitaller (a fellow military order). At the end of the day, the Master of the Hospitallers and the Marshal of the Templars lay dead on the battlefield.

Not far away, at Saffuriya, the army of Jerusalem stood ready to meet the Saracens. Unfortunately, they were under the command of King Guy I – the same Guy of Lusignan who had killed the Earl of Salisbury and others in his attempt to kidnap Queen Eleanor. Militarily incompetent and constantly vacillating, the king was persuaded by Raymond of Tripoli to stand his ground and let the larger army of Saladin advance against him. However, after a late night visit from Gerard of Ridefort, the Master of the Knights Templar, he changed his mind and, the next morning, ordered his army to advance to relieve the town of Tiberias, which was under siege by Saladin. Although less than 20 miles away, Tiberias could only be reached by marching across dust-dry country, which soon exhausted the mail-clad soldiers of the Christian army. To the constant, unrelenting heat, had to be added the scourge of Saracen mounted bowmen, who raced in and loosed their arrows at the trudging soldiers – especially at the Knights Templar contingent who were bringing up the rear. With no water for men or horses, Guy decided to pitch camp close to two large hills known as the Horns of Hattin. The next morning, the Christians awoke to find themselves surrounded by Saladin's troops. By the end of the day, Guy was Saladin's prisoner, all the Templars, with the strange exception of the Grand Master, who was released, were dead (with 230 executed after the battle), and a piece of the True Cross, brought onto the battlefield by the now-dead Bishop of Acre, was in the hands of the infidel. Before long, Tiberias fell, soon followed by the coastal towns of Acre and Ascalon. Only Jerusalem remained and, after a siege of less than two weeks, surrender terms were agreed. To have stuck it out to the bitter end would have ensured a massacre of the city's residents; instead they would have to pay a large ransom for their lives.

When the news reached western Europe, the shock of defeat was magnified by the feeling of outrage that, not only were the Saracens now desecrating the Holy Sepulchre, they had in their possession a piece of the True Cross. The Pope, Urban III, died, it was said, of a broken heart. His successor, Gregory VIII, whilst demanding a new Crusade, also believed that all Christians should be punished, as the loss of the Holy City was clearly a response to their many sins. Accordingly, he decided that all Christians should fast on Fridays and go without meat on Wednesdays and Saturdays for the next five years.

Saladin. (By Gustave Doré)

On hearing the news, Prince Richard immediately took up the Cross and prepared to go on Crusade. Henry II and the new King of France, Phillip II, took the Cross in January 1188, but by June the same year were at war with each other. Even more depressing for Henry was the fact that Richard had allied himself with Phillip. Forced to leave his base at Le Mans, Henry left with Phillip and Richard close behind. In command of the rearguard was William FitzJohn, once ransomed by Eleanor and now high in the king's estimate as a doughty and loyal fighter. So high, in fact, that FitzJohn, a younger son of a minor baron, had been promised in marriage to the daughter and heir of the Earl of Pembroke.

As he watched from the rear of Henry's retreating army, FitzJohn saw a figure racing on horseback in his direction. It proved to be Richard who, inexplicably, was not wearing his chain mail armour. When Richard realised that it was FitzJohn who he was bearing down upon, he pulled back on his reins and shouted to the knight asking him not to charge at him as he was without armour. At this, FitzJohn lowered his lance and rode straight at the prince. Just as Richard thought his time had come, FitzJohn lowered his lance further and killed Richard's horse.

During the first days of July, it became clear that Henry had been beaten by the combination of Phillip and Richard. He was summoned from his castle at Chinon to hear the demands of the King of France. After resting at the Knights Templar property at Ballan, he met with Phillip and Richard. Amongst their demands was one insisting that he take no revenge against his own barons who had sided with his enemy. When the list of names of the renegades was produced, Henry learned to his absolute shock that the first name on the list was his favourite son, Prince John.

Carried back to Chinon, Henry became weaker by the hour. Finally, exhausted and wracked with grief at the defeat he had suffered, Henry II of England died on 6 July 1189.

William FitzJohn sent word to Richard who, in turn, sent FitzJohn to release the 67-year-old Queen Eleanor from her sixteen-year confinement. Armed with letters brought by FitzJohn from Richard, Eleanor raced up to London, where she was to act as regent in her son's absence. Her main task was to ensure the loyalty of the English barons, and in this she succeeded admirably.

Richard was crowned in Westminster Abbey on Sunday 3 September 1189. With his coronation out of the way, Richard set about raising funds for the forthcoming Crusade. To his shock, he found that the Royal Treasury at Winchester was practically bare. Furthermore, the special 'Saladin Tithe', which had been introduced by Henry, had all been handed over to the Templars and had either been used in Henry's war against Phillip and Richard, or was now part of the Church of Rome's general Crusading fund and was, therefore, no longer available. In addition, Henry had sent 30,000 marks for the improvement of the defences of the city of Tyre. In a storm of economic activity, Richard put up for sale all his property in England. Every office that was in his power to grant was revoked until the holder (or some higher bidder) had repurchased it. The chancellorship – once proudly owned by Thomas Becket – went for sale at £3,000. Towns and cities were invited to bid for new charters, and monasteries vied to purchase new privileges. Even King William I of Scotland found that, for a mere 10,000 marks, he could buy his release from his vassalage to Richard.

Oddly enough, with such fundraising taking place, there appears to be no source which suggests that Richard went to the most obvious place of all to obtain funds. The Knights Templar were awash with money and yet it seems that Richard never applied to them for help or, if he did, he does not appear to have been successful. What can be certain, however, is that Richard and the Templars achieved a remarkable closeness during the forthcoming Crusade.

Phillip and Richard were joined on the Crusade by Frederick I (Barbarossa), the Holy Roman Emperor. Frederick set off in May 1189, taking the overland route to the Holy Land in company with a huge Crusader army. The two kings decided to go by sea, although not together. To improve their protection whilst passing through the Mediterranean, both Phillip and Richard paid the Doge of Genoa for the privilege of flying the Genoese flag – a red cross on a white background. In 1188 it had been agreed by Henry and Phillip (before they resumed their casual war against each other) that, in an effort to distinguish the Crusader armies, a cross would be worn on their tunics. Phillip opted for a red cross on a white background; Henry accepted a white cross on a red background, and Phillip of Flanders chose a green cross on a white background. Later, Frederick's Germans would choose a white cross on a black background. At some future date, the French and the English exchanged crosses and the red cross on a white background – the flag of St George of Genoa – and the emblem of the Knights Templar, was to become the flag of England. This may have come about when the Templars were involved in manning the royal ships. In December 1226 Henry III's records mention 'Brother Thomas, Templar, who was accustomed to command the king's great ship'. It is not too fanciful to imagine that Brother Thomas would have flown the Templars' flag of a red cross on a white background whilst in command of the king's great ship (St George's cross remains the personal flag of an admiral in the Royal Navy). In many subsequent pictures depicting King Richard he is shown dressed as a Templar, and he is known, on at least one occasion, to have been disguised as a Templar.

The Third Crusade proved to be a mass of conflicting interests and squabbles. Isaac Angelus, the Emperor of Constantinople, had agreed with Saladin that he would impede the path of the Germans as they came overland. This led to the grabbing of hostages and the seizure of land before Isaac relented and allowed the Germans across the Dardanelles. Shortly afterwards, it hardly seemed worth the effort when the German emperor drowned whilst swimming in a river. This persuaded many of the Germans to pack up and go home, leaving those who remained to come under the command of Duke Leopold of Austria.

Conrad of Montferrat was contesting the kingship of Jerusalem with King Guy and had refused Guy entry to Tyre. Guy promptly took himself off and besieged Acre, where he not only had little success against the fortress, but also had Saladin attacking his rear. During this siege, Gerard de Ridefort, the Grand Master of the Templars, who had escaped with his life at the Horns of Hattin, was killed.

Richard arrived at Messina in Sicily and found himself embroiled in a war against the ruler, Tancred, who was holding Joan, Richard's sister and wife of the previous ruler. Furthermore, Tancred was holding on to a legacy that should have gone to Richard's father, Henry II. After a couple of swift, punishing defeats (during which Phillip, also on Sicily, just stood by and watched), Tancred capitulated and paid Richard 20,000 gold ounces with another 20,000 to Joan as a portion of her late husband's estate.

Joan was taken to a ship which was carrying Princess Berengaria of Navarre. The princess had been brought out by Richard's mother, Eleanor, and it was intended that he would marry her in the Holy Land. A little awkwardness was introduced by the fact that Richard was supposed to marry Phillip's sister Alice, but the French princess had been seduced by Henry, Richard's father. This had not endeared her to Eleanor, who had taken it upon herself to find a bride for her son.

With her job done, Eleanor returned to Aquitaine, but not before telling Richard that his brother John was careering around England acting as if he was the king. In this, even

John was outdone by the regent Richard had left in charge, William Longchamp, who had grown high and mighty in his new position.

When the English fleet sailed from Messina, it ran into a storm and several ships were wrecked off the coast of Cyprus. The self-styled 'Emperor of Cyprus', Isaac Comnenus, promptly stole all the treasure held in the ships and took the survivors off for ransom. Richard, forced to respond to this outrage, landed and captured the entire island – something for which he had not planned. Richard and Berengaria were married at Limassol on 12 May 1191.

Four weeks after Richard and his new bride's arrival at Acre, the Muslim defenders sued for peace. In consultation with Saladin, camped nearby, the terms included the payment of 200,000 gold pieces, the release of 1,500 Christian prisoners and the return of the relic of the True Cross. The French king took over the citadel for his accommodation and Richard joined the Templars at their headquarters overlooking the sea. When the royal standards were run up, Richard was annoyed to see the flag of Leopold, Duke of Austria, flying above the city. As Richard considered the German contingent to have done very little in the battle for the fortress, he tore the flag down and threw it into the moat. The bloodshed threatened by this act was only avoided when the Templars stepped in and separated the English and German soldiers. The next day, the duke and the German contingent left to go home.

King Phillip followed not long after, his enthusiasm for crusading much diminished by the realities of the campaign. Richard was probably not sorry to see him go as he had not proved to be much of a military commander. He had, nevertheless, left his troops behind under the command of the Duke of Burgundy. On the other hand, the French king would be at liberty to cause problems for Richard once he arrived back in Paris.

King Richard and King Phillip accept the keys to Acre.

The island of Cyprus was also proving to be something of a problem. The Greek Orthodox people of the island had shown themselves to be less than welcoming to the 'Latins', and the thought of a revolt to his rear as he advanced towards Jerusalem was unsettling. The solution was to sell the island to the Knights Templar, which was done for 100,000 gold dinars. Even this proved to be more difficult than expected, and on one occasion, fifteen knights, twenty-nine other horsemen and seventy-four foot soldiers found themselves besieged in Nicosia Castle by thousands of angry islanders. Rather than face death by starvation, the Templars decided to attack from the castle. After Mass on Easter Sunday morning, the gates were flung open and the Templars charged out, scattering the besiegers. Panic broke out and the rebels fled, many falling to the lances and swords of the Templars. Eventually, the island was resold, this time to Guy Lusignan, still calling himself 'King of Jerusalem' even though it had been decided that the crown should go to Henry, Count of Champagne; the other candidate, Conrad of Montferrat, had been murdered.

One distinctly strange aspect of the Templars at this time was the appointment of Robert de Sable as their Grand Master. After the death of de Ridefort, no one had been appointed Grand Master for almost a year. It has been suggested that this delay was caused by concern amongst the knights that the tradition of their Grand Master being at the forefront of battle should be re-examined. This policy, although noble in concept, actually placed the Templar leadership at constant risk. The twice-married de Sable had never been a Templar, but within months of being initiated he was placed at the head of the Order. A possible reason for this may be found in the fact that one of his great-aunts – Jeanne de Sable – had married Hughes, Baron de Mathefelon, a knight of Champagne. The Mathefelons were a powerful and well-connected family, and any Champagne connection was very useful in association with the Knights Templar. Oddly enough, Hughes' great-grandmother was Heldegarde de Beaugency. She was known as 'Lancelotte' – the female version of 'Lancelot'. Her close male relatives were named 'Lancelin', again an early version of 'Lancelot'.

Aware that the campaigning season was advancing, Richard was keen to move south and set himself up for an attack on Jerusalem. Frustrated by Saladin's prevarications over the terms of the surrender of Acre, and angered by reports that the Saracens' leader had executed a number of his Christian prisoners, Richard ordered the execution of his Muslim hostages.

In full view of Saladin's army, somewhere between 2,000 and 3,000 Islamic warriors lost their heads (a horrifying total, although a small number when compared to the Persian massacre of up to 90,000 Christians after the capture of Jerusalem in AD 614). After the executions, the bodies were opened up to retrieve any gold or jewels that had been swallowed. Gall bladders were also taken from the bodies as it was believed that, by swallowing the bile contained in the bladders, warriors would become much more aggressive ('bilious' or 'choleric').

The Crusader army set off from Acre at the end of August 1191 to cover the 70 miles to Jaffa, which Richard intended to use as a base for his assault on Jerusalem. Thousands of knights and foot soldiers formed a column that stretched along the coast. To their seaward side, the baggage train trundled along protected by the main army. Out at sea, Richard's ships kept pace and sent ashore supplies as required. On the landward side, Saladin's army marched a parallel course, grasping every opportunity to shower arrows on the Crusaders in the hope of goading them into a retaliatory foray. In the vanguard of the column rode the Knights Templar – this was always their position when serving with Richard; in battle they formed his right wing. The rear of the column was guarded by the black-mantled Knights Hospitaller.

Failing to provoke the Crusaders, Saladin decided to force a battle near the ruined town of Arsuf. On 7 September, with the Saracens in battle formation ahead of him, and to a background of Saracen kettledrums and blaring trumpets, Richard sent word down the column to prepare for battle.

Saladin's plan was to attack at several points in the hope of breaking up the Christian army. To Richard, however, it was vital that his men stayed together in a tight formation and, in the beginning, the Christian soldiers stood their ground. With his initial tactics failing to produce results, Saladin changed to an all-out assault on the rear of the column. Under great pressure, the Master of the Hospitallers requested permission from Richard to charge the enemy; Richard refused. Finally, provoked beyond endurance, and seeing the enemy bowmen dismounting to discharge their arrows more accurately, the Hospitallers charged, followed by the French knights.

Seeing this, Richard's options were limited. He could go to the aid of his rearguard, risking the break-up of the remaining column and its piecemeal destruction, or he could remain in formation and suffer the probable loss of the Hospitallers and the French. Richard decided to attack and sent the Breton and Angevin knights on a charge against the enemy, whilst he led the Templars, the Norman and English knights in a charge at Saladin's centre and left. Inspired by Richard's example, the Christians drove at all before them, only to find 700 mounted warriors of Saladin's personal bodyguard bearing down on the Christian left flank. Alerted to the danger, Richard rallied his knights and, again at their head, charged straight at the oncoming Saracens. The Muslim horsemen, expecting an enemy flight at their approach, now faced a solid phalanx of knights, spearheaded with the iron points of their lances, charging directly at them. This was exactly what the Knights Templar were trained for, and their fellow knights were keen not to be outshone. After the first terrible shock of brutal contact, the Saracens were scattered and soon all of Saladin's army was in flight.

Richard's victory at Arsuf had not matched Saladin's at the Horns of Hattin, but it had shown that Saladin could be beaten. And Richard had left his personal mark on the conflict between Christianity and Islam – from then on, Muslim children who misbehaved were warned that if they did not improve, they could expect a visit from the dreadful 'Malik Ric' – King Richard.

By January 1192, Richard had reached within 12 miles of Jerusalem, only to turn back when it became clear that, in the prevailing weather conditions of cold and rain, a long siege would be an unattractive proposition. An attempt to seek a peaceful outcome by proposing the marriage of his widowed sister Joan to Saladin's brother came to nothing, much to the delight of the uninformed and outraged widow.

After moving south to Ascalon, Richard mounted another attempt against Jerusalem, encouraged by the discovery of yet another piece of the True Cross and the pillaging of an extremely rich Muslim caravan his army encountered on its way. This time, the Lionheart reached to within 5 miles of the city, but, when it came into view, legend says that he covered his eyes that he might not gaze upon the glittering prize until he could take it for Christ. Once again, persuaded by the commanders of his forces (who were keen to attack Egypt before Jerusalem), Richard turned back to Ascalon. Once there, he discovered that Saladin had attacked Jaffa. Taking just 50 knights, 300 archers and a similar number of foot soldiers, Richard arrived at the port where, at first glance, it seemed certain that the fortress had fallen. He learned, however, that the citadel was still holding out and, leading his men ashore, scattered the Saracens who had been distracted by the opportunity to loot the city.

A few days later, the rising sun saw Saladin's army moving forward to mount an attack against the citadel. Rallying his men, Richard, his bodyguard of a dozen Knights Templar and a few of his archers and foot soldiers, came out to face the enemy. Charging furiously up and down the Saracen lines, Richard raised his battleaxe and roared defiance at the Muslim troops who, finding themselves face to face with a terrifying legend, started to fall back. Within a short time, the entire invading army was in retreat.

A month of negotiations followed. With Richard concerned about rumours that his brother John was causing problems in England, and that Phillip was preparing to invade Normandy, and with Saladin's army exhausted, a compromise was sought by both sides. Eventually, a three-year truce was agreed whereby the Christians could retain all their coastal territories from

Tyre to Jaffa, and pilgrims could travel in safety to visit the holy sites in Jerusalem. In return, Ascalon had to be given up and would be destroyed. Although the truce was welcomed by the Christians, it was probably a mistake. Within six months Saladin was dead and, with no obvious successor, divisions amongst the Saracens would have laid the Holy City wide open to attack.

As it was, Richard left Acre disguised as a Knight Templar in company with four other Templars. After an adventurous voyage, including a run-in with pirates off Corfu, the small party was wrecked on the shore north of Venice. This was dangerous territory as the land was part of the German emperor's domain, and the emperor, Henry VI, was no friend of Richard's after the Lionheart had made an agreement with Tancred of Sicily against Henry. A long westward route would bring Richard to the French border, but he knew he would get no assistance in that quarter. On the other hand, by heading north-east in the direction of Vienna, he could cross over into Bohemia or Moravia, both of whom were vassals to his brother-in-law, Henry the Lion, Duke of Saxony and Bavaria, and none of them were admirers of the German emperor. There remained, however, a problem. Before reaching the borders of his brother-in-law's vassals, Richard would have to pass through Austria, ruled by Duke Leopold, still smarting from having his standard thrown into the moat at Acre by Richard.

Disguised as pilgrims, Richard and two of the Templar knights set off for Vienna. Staying at an inn just outside the city, within 50 miles of the Moravian border, their over-exuberant spending was brought to the attention of the local authorities. As a result, just before Christmas 1192, Richard found himself in the hands of a vengeful Duke Leopold. Two months later, the duke negotiated a deal with the German emperor to sell Richard to him for 75,000 marks.

When word reached England of Richard's capture, two abbots were sent to find him and to find out what the inevitable demands would be. The king was found on his way to Speyer, where he was to be tried for allying himself with the emperor's enemies. There the abbots were joined by Hubert Walter, Bishop of Salisbury, who had been with Richard in the Holy Land and had even defended Acre against besieging Saracens. As a result, Richard had decided that Bishop Walter should be the next to take the post of Archbishop of Canterbury, which was currently vacant.

At his trial, Richard defended himself so well that the emperor rushed to give him the kiss of peace and promised to do all he could to bring about a reconciliation between Richard and Phillip of France. In the meantime, however, there still remained the small question of a ransom to be paid. Henry decided that the amount should be enough to serve as a severe lesson, enough to almost bring England and its European provinces to their knees. He decided that the cost of ransoming the king should be 100,000 marks – equivalent to 35 tons of pure silver.

When the news arrived in England, Richard's mother, Eleanor, immediately set about raising the money. Whereas the Saladin Tithe had been set at 10 per cent, Richard's release demanded 25 per cent. Churches were ordered to hand over their Communion silver and even the crosses from their altars. Gervase of Canterbury wrote of demands for 'church chalices, containers, crosses and candlesticks', whilst Ralph de Diceto recorded the handing over of 'silver chalices from parish churches'. Monasteries with little worldly wealth were to hand over at least one year's income from their sheep. Eleanor knew there was no time to waste, for word had come that her other son, John, and the King of France were attempting to raise funds to have Richard kept in German detention.

Eventually, 75 per cent of the ransom was raised, the figure at which the German emperor had agreed to release Richard if noble hostages could be found to take his place until the remainder was paid. Amongst the hostages was Hugh de

Despite being disguised, King Richard is captured.

Morville, the leading murderer of Thomas Becket. He took with him a copy of the Arthurian tales, which was used by a Swiss priest, Ulrich von Zatzikhoven, to produce his own poem, *Lanzelet*, based on the story of Lancelot.

True to medieval form, Richard lost his life five years later in a minor squabble over the discovery of buried treasure. Immediately taking to arms to sort out the problem, Richard closed on the castle at Chalus-Chabrol in the Limousin. A close reconnoitre beneath the castle walls brought Richard within crossbow range, and a bolt shot from the castle struck him in the left shoulder. After publicly forgiving the soldier who had brought him down, Richard died of gangrene eleven days later. At his bedside was Eleanor, his 77-year-old mother. Among the first she told of his death was William FitzJohn, now holder of the hereditary title Marshal of England (and who would be known from now on as 'William the Marshal', or simply 'William Marshal'). The faithful knight who, like the king, was almost certainly a Knights Templar confrere, received from Richard the governorship of the city of Rouen and the responsibility for the royal treasure, most of which was in the Templar vaults.

Above left: 1. A Knight Templar.

Above right: 2. The unearthing of the Lance.

3. A medieval picture of Christ showing his lance wound to God, who is holding a chalice filled with blood.

Above left: 4. King Henry II of England.

Above right: 5. Bernard of Clairvaux.

Left: 6. Becket's death. FitzUrse, recognisable from the bear design on his shield, strikes at Becket, as de Tracy injures Brother Grim.

7. A side panel of a Becket reliquary. A golden (gilded?) chalice stands prominent on the altar.

8. At the Battle of Camlann, Arthur charges at Mordred. An early twentieth-century representation.

Above: 9. Sir Percival as a 'Red Cross' knight. (Painting by Ferdinand Leeke, 1812)

Opposite above: 10. Medieval tile from Chertsey Abbey showing Richard the Lionheart.

Opposite below: 11. King Phillip and King Richard argue during the Crusade.

Left: 12. King John.

Below: 13. A fourteenth-century illustration of the Lance and the Holy Grail being paraded before King Arthur. The arbitrary addition of a lid for the Grail is commonplace in medieval art.

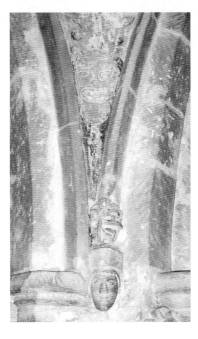

Above left: 14. The carved head, acanthus leaves, and the image of the imp in Nettleham church.

Above right: 15. Robert Kilwardby, Dominican Archbishop of Canterbury.

Left: 16. An early twentieth-century design by S.E. Gay titled 'The Great Master'. It shows Christ standing triumphant on an overthrown and broken Cross. The Knights Templar may well have approved.

Above left: 17. A panel from a medieval stained-glass window shows a golden chalice receiving the sacrificial blood of the Lamb of God, the lamb standing beneath a pennant bearing the red cross of a martyr.

Above right: 18. The coat of arms of the city of Lincoln.

Above left: 19. An eighteenth-century statue bringing together three of the key elements in the story of the Holy Grail – the Blessed Virgin, the Cross and the Chalice.

Above right: 20. The chalice found in the tomb of Bishop Sutton.

8

THE MURDER OF
KING JOHN

Whilst King John had inherited much of his father's administrative abilities, there was little in his make-up regarding kingship. Named 'Lackland' for his failure to obtain lands of his own, either from his father or from his brother, when the opportunity to govern did come along, he managed to ruin it.

In 1177 Henry II had made the 11-year-old John the King of Ireland. Eight years later, it was decided John should be knighted and sent to rule his previously unvisited kingdom. Greeted courteously by the Irish chieftains, John, in company with his fellow courtiers, publicly ridiculed the dignitaries, scorning their dress and manners. Then, within a very short time, he ejected the chiefs from their castles and gave the properties to his friends. Six months after his arrival, his father dragged him back to England, annoyed by his behaviour.

The death of Richard showed that little in John's demeanour had changed. During High Mass at Fontevroux, a day or so after Richard had been buried in the abbey, John continually interrupted the sermon being given by Bishop Hugh of Lincoln with the complaint that he was hungry. Eventually, the bishop ordered him to leave.

Instead of complaining about an empty stomach, John would have been better employed at countering the revolt that had broken out in his newly inherited lands in Brittany. There, Arthur, the son of his brother Geoffrey, was considered to be the real heir to the throne. As John was being boorish with Bishop Hugh, Arthur, in company with Phillip of France, was marching on Angers, the ancient seat of the Angevins.

On hearing this, John dashed to Le Mans, the capital of his county of Maine, only to flee when he found that rebels were advancing against the city. Within days, Arthur was giving homage to the French king for Anjou, Maine and the county of Touraine, with its capital at Tours.

John then headed for Rouen where he crowned himself Duke of Normandy. The ceremony was not only meagre, but was also spoiled by the oafish behaviour of John and his courtiers. At one stage, when being presented with the Ducal Lance, John dropped it, much to the hilarity of himself and his followers.

With his empire collapsing around him, John had his ten-year marriage to his wife, Isabelle of Gloucester, annulled. With this achieved, he could now marry the 12-year-old Isabella of Angoulême. The chief problem with this idea was that the young woman was betrothed to Hugh le Brun of Lusignan. Not only was this the same family who had tried to kidnap Eleanor many years earlier, but Hugh had actually kidnapped the elderly queen only a short time before. Her release was obtained after just a few hours of captivity, but at the cost of the county of La Marche.

An appeal to Phillip by the Lusignans failed when the French king became embroiled in a complex network of relationships with women. The situation had become so difficult that the Pope had placed an interdict upon France, thus denying the use of churches to the population. However, once his problems were solved (with the sudden death of one of the women), Phillip turned on John with a vengeance. Demanding that the King of England appear at a tribunal in France, Phillip was met with a blank refusal. His response was to hand all of John's possessions on the Continent over to Arthur – with the exception of Normandy, which he intended to keep for himself.

In turn, John responded by taking an army across the Channel, where they found Arthur besieging his grandmother at Mirebeau. Taken by surprise, Arthur was captured and imprisoned at Falaise. There, the young man was guarded by Hubert de Burgh, who was appalled when John sent orders for Arthur to be blinded and otherwise mutilated to ensure he could no longer challenge the king for the throne. De Burgh sent the messengers away and refused to allow the orders to be carried out. John then ordered that Arthur be taken to Rouen where he came under the guardianship of William de Braose – one of John's inner circle. In April 1203 Arthur mysteriously disappeared, never to be seen again. Inevitably, on all sides, John was seen as the cause of Arthur's disappearance, but although rumours rampaged, none were ever proved.

The most immediate result of all this warlike activity was the desperate need for funds. John became notorious in his frequent – indeed, almost constant – raising of taxes. One of his chroniclers (admittedly hostile), Matthew Paris, described the king as 'an insatiable extorter of money, an invader and wrecker of the possessions of his subjects'. When some of his barons showed reluctance in joining one of his Continental wars, he mustered them at Portsmouth, took the money they had provided for themselves as expenses and spent it on recruiting mercenaries.

The Church proved to be more of a problem. In the early part of his reign, John blundered by insisting that the Cistercians pay taxes. When they refused to pay without the authorisation of the Cistercian General Chapter, he banned them from grazing their sheep and cattle on royal lands. Almost immediately he was forced to back down, but somehow, his foresters and land agents had not been told of the decision. During a meeting at Lincoln, at which the King of Scotland vowed to be his vassal, John was approached by twelve Cistercian abbots who complained about the lack of access to the land. The king promptly knelt in front of them and begged for forgiveness. He agreed to their requests and promised to build an abbey at Beaulieu in compensation and to supply it with cattle and an annual stock of wine.

In 1207 the king, yet again, showed a weakness in the face of the Church. With heavy costs arising from his warring on the Continent, he demanded a tax on both clergy and laity. When the clergy displayed opposition to the new tax, John promptly withdrew the demand. Just two years later, however, in a squabble over who had the right to appoint the Archbishop of Canterbury, John found himself excommunicated by the Pope and with an interdict placed on the whole of England. Now, with no reason to be wary of the Church's power, the king sold off the Archbishop of Canterbury's property, and income from the clergy rose from £400 to £24,000 in two years. Even the Cistercians came under pressure and were forced to pay large amounts of money to the king. As for the Jews in England, every means possible was used to extract money from them.

John also raised taxes from another organisation, but had to be very careful in his handling of its relationship with the Crown. The Knights Templar, with their headquarters at the Temple in London, and with preceptories throughout England, were unquestionably the financial power-brokers in the realm. Early in his reign, John had deposited the Crown jewels in the Temple, ostensibly for them to 'guard', but in reality as security for loans. Money owed to the king would be paid to the Temple and money owed by the king would be paid by the Templars on his behalf. Because of their ability to cross borders without molestation, money could be sent across front lines in war. Examples of this occurred when, having lost much of his Continental lands to King Phillip, John was able to set up trusts by which the Templars paid pensions to his displaced vassals in order to retain their loyalty. The Templars were also given the responsibility of paying an allowance to John's sister-in-law, Richard's wife, Berengaria. Money was borrowed to pay ransom fees and to pay off other debtors.

Nevertheless, the Templars were not a charity and, whilst usury (the charging of interest on a loan) was forbidden to Christians, they side-stepped the problem by charging fees for the services they rendered. Inevitably, the fees charged against John mounted throughout his reign. So deep in debt did he become that, on the day the Pope's excommunication was lifted (at the Templar church at Dover), he had to borrow a single gold mark from the Templars to make an offering to the Church. But it was to get much worse, and burgeoning conflicts led to the loans of much larger sums. This increasing debt caused the Templars to keep the king closely under their observation, to the extent that during the last four years of his reign, John frequently stayed at the Temple whilst he was in London. Also, during his conflict with the barons that resulted in the Magna Carta, the Master of the English Templars, Aymeric de St Maur, was not only amongst his closest advisors, but was also one of the signatories of the document.

There may have been an even better reason to keep a close eye on the king. According to the chronicler Matthew Paris, who claimed to have heard the story from a fellow monk who was actually involved, towards the end of his excommunication, King John sent a delegation to the Emir of Morocco with an offer to place England under Sharia law with himself converting to Islam. The emir, however, refused to have anything to do with a sovereign who would so disgrace himself as to give away his people and his country. It has to be admitted that Paris was not a great admirer of John, but when the story was published, there was no great rebuttal or censorship from any authority or position close to the Crown. If there had been any truth, or even a suggestion of truth, in the matter, the Knights Templar would have been keen to watch the king closely, and to take any action that they – and the Church – deemed necessary.

In the event, it can certainly be said that John surrendered England to the Pope and became a papal vassal in 1213, much to the annoyance of his barons.

After the signing of the Magna Carta in June 1215, John applied to the Pope to have the document annulled on the grounds that he had signed it under duress. The Pope agreed. After all, England was now one of his vassal states and, although his own Knights Templar had approved of the signing, he had not been consulted. John promptly began to recruit mercenaries on the Continent. One of the contingents crossing the English Channel was shipwrecked and the bodies of many women and children were strewn along English beaches. The idea that the mercenaries were coming with their families gave rise to the rapidly expanding rumour that John's forces intended to repopulate the country after a massacre of its citizens.

Rebel barons rallied at London and decided that the only way they could counter John's mercenaries was to invite the French king to come to their aid. Phillip, however, was not keen, but, in agreement with his son, Prince Louis, he sent detachments of French knights in support of the English barons. In the meantime, John inexplicably decided to ignore the barons in London and set off on a countrywide rampage, only agreeing to hold back his mercenaries from despoiling towns and villages on the payment of large sums of money. Captured rebel supporters were held for ransom. By early 1216, the king had reached as far north as the Firth of Forth before turning back to spread devastation in the east of England.

Once again, the rebel barons asked King Phillip for help. In response, the Pope sent a cardinal to Phillip to remind him that England was now a papal vassal state and any attack upon John was an attack upon the Pope. Phillip countered by arguing that John had acted as a traitor whilst his own brother was held prisoner by the Emperor of Germany; therefore, he could not be considered a legitimate sovereign and could not have given England to the Pope. Even if he had been King of England by right, he had forfeited that right by murdering his nephew, Arthur. Furthermore, he had acted, in giving away his country, without the approval of his barons. No matter which way the problem was viewed, King John had no right to cede his realm to the Pope. Prince Louis' case was even simpler. By giving the Crown of England to the Pope, John had resigned from the throne. The English barons had invited Louis to come to their aid, so they were clearly looking for a new king, and he – Louis – would be happy to oblige.

The French prince and his army landed in Kent in the third week of May. Instead of immediately opposing the invasion, John withdrew, because he could not trust the French mercenaries in his ranks. Retreating to the west, the king allowed the French to take London without opposition and, in company with the rebel barons, spread as far south as Winchester and as far north as Lincoln. At the latter city, Gilbert of Ghent, a Lincolnshire rebel, was valiantly fended off by an opposition led by a widow, Nicola de la Haye.

Alarmed by news that King Alexander of Scotland had brought an army south and intended to link up with Louis, John set off from Corfe Castle in July and headed northwards. He took with him an extraordinary baggage train. The previous month, the king had instructed the Templars and others that he wanted all the royal possessions held in their treasuries to be returned to him. Now his wagons lurched beneath the weight of hundreds of precious vessels of every shape and size, from cups to basins. Jewellery, combs, candelabras, altar crosses and shrines rattled along with a set of English Crown jewels and another set that had belonged to the Empress Matilda. Amongst other relics, there was even the sword of Tristram, a relic of an Arthurian hero.

The hoard of treasure followed John as he reached Lincoln (missing Alexander's return to Scotland) and he pursued his enemies through the rest of Lincolnshire. Having stamped his authority on the local dissenters, the king entered Norfolk and stayed at Lynn where the people, wary of the damage his mercenaries had done to their northern neighbour, made an effort to make him welcome. But the king was not finished. On 11 October 1216 John set out again for Lincolnshire. Skirting the Wash, he spent a night at Wisbech before turning north the following day towards Sutton St Mary, then westwards towards Spalding. Behind the king, as he left Lynn, was his baggage train. Travelling at a much slower rate, the wagons were soon left behind and they and their escort were never seen again.

The usual answer to this mystery lies in a claim that whoever was leading the baggage train decided to cross the clearly treacherous mud-flats of a southerly arm of the Wash whilst the tide was out. If this was the case, it must have been amongst the most absurd decisions taken in history. Quite obviously, the proposed journey would have been fraught with appalling risk under ordinary means of passage, but to try and do it with pack animals, horses, oxen and wagons, especially with a particularly heavy load, would have been unthinkable. Apart from the vast stretches of mud and quicksand, there was always the risk of the tide returning. It is true that guides existed to take people across the muddy wastes, but even they would not know of a route that could support such a lumbering, cumbersome and – on mud – unmanageable load. After the disappearance of the baggage train, no wreckage was found;

no bodies, no flotsam and there were no local tales of sudden wealth amongst those who lived on the banks of the Wash. And yet, strangely, some of the treasure was to reappear in due course, recognised, but without comment. It is also worthy of note that there are no records of any search at all being mounted for the baggage train. It is hardly comprehensible that such a vast fortune should have been allowed to be lost without any effort at its recovery – unless, of course, no one believed that it had been lost.

Yet, if amongst the relics demanded by John before setting out for Lincolnshire there had been a gilded chalice, which was believed to be the cup used by Christ at the Last Supper and by Joseph of Arimathea to catch Christ's blood at the Crucifixion, there was one group who may have had good reason to take a close interest in the baggage train. The Knights Templar, to whom John was deeply in debt, owed the king no personal or group loyalty. Their loyalty remained with the Church. They had been taxed heavily by the king, as had their brethren in the Cistercian monasteries. Although John had awarded the kingdom to the Pope, it was equally in his nature to take it back again – especially once the French had been removed from English soil. A new Pope (Honorius III) had just been enthroned who, although professing continued support for the king, may, in the style of Henry II, have indicated to the Templars a different response. Furthermore, there was always the suggestion that John had previously tried to turn England into a Muslim state. Such an act would have earned the undying enmity of the Templars.

It would not have been difficult for the Templars to have taken the treasure. They could have taken it by force of arms as it approached the banks of the Wash, or even have had the escort provided covertly by Templar knights and sergeants. Both could have been arranged by the leading figure in John's army – William Marshal, the Earl of Pembroke and Marshal of

England – a Templar confrere who had already vowed to die as a Knight Templar. Earlier the same William Marshal, as a result of John's unfounded malice, had been deprived of much of his land and castles, and had been forced to hand over his sons as hostages to the king.

Whatever the method used, the baggage train disappeared. If amongst the treasures was the gilded chalice, it was now back in Templar hands and, like parts of the Crown jewels, to reappear at a later date.

There still remained the problem of the king. With much of his reign utterly mismanaged, he had brought an interdiction on his people and excommunication on himself. He had brought about a civil war and an invasion of French forces. His taxes had forced his barons against him and drained the wealth of the Cistercians. It is suggested that, after the loss of his baggage train, John spent a few nights at the monastery at Swineshead, suffering from dysentery, before leaving for the Bishop of Lincoln's castle at Newark where, in answer to the problem, he died.

There are, however, several sources that disagree with this conclusion to John's life: Walter of Hemingford (better known as Walter of Guisborough), William Caxton, William Shakespeare, Foxes' *Book of Martyrs* and local tradition – a source often ignored by historians at their peril.

According to Walter of Hemingford, the king, on hearing that the abbot had an attractive sister serving as a prioress close by, demanded to see her. The monastery's hospitaller (the brother responsible for the health of the monks) asked the abbot to 'absolve me father, and pray for me, and I will rid the earth of this monster'. The hospitaller then presented the king with poisoned pears, thus causing his death.

Caxton wrote that the king, after discovering that corn was cheap in the area, 'answered that he would ere long make it so dear, that a penny loaf would be sold for a shilling'. At this, a lay monk named Simon took poison from a toad, added it to a cup of wine and drank some before offering the cup to the king. John took the cup and drained it. The monk died almost immediately, and the king two days later.

In his play, *King John*, William Shakespeare actually has the king saying: 'Our abbeys and our priories shall pay this expedition's charge'. In Act V, Scene VI, Hubert de Burgh informs Philip the Bastard of the king's condition:

Hubert	The king, I fear, is poison'd by a monk:
	I left him almost speechless, and broke out
	To acquaint you with this evil, that you might
	The better arm you to the sudden time
	Than if you had of leisure known of this.
Bastard	How did he take it? Who did taste to him?
Hubert	A monk, I tell you; a resolved villain,
	Whose bowels suddenly burst out: the king
	Yet speaks and peradventure may recover.

In 1570 Lincolnshire-born John Foxe published an edition of his 'Actes and Monuments of these latter and perillous Dayes' (The *Book of Martyrs*) which contained the following:

as kyng John was come to Swinestead Abbey, not farre from Lincolne; he rested there two dayes: where as moste writers testifie, he was most traiterouslye poisoned by a monke of the abbey, of the sect of the Cistercians or S. Bernard's brethren called Simon of Swinsted.

Foxe then goes into detail:

The foresaid monke Simon being much offended with certaine talke that the kyng had at hys table, concernyge Lodovicke the French kyngs sonne (which had then entred and usurped upon him) dyd cast in hys

wycked hart how he most spedily might bryng him to his ende. And
first of all he counselled with his Abbot, shewing him the whole matter,
and what he was minded to do. He alledged for himselfe the prophecy
of Cayphas, John. xi. saying: It is better that one man dye, then all the
people should perish. I am well contented (sayth he) to loose my lyfe,
and so become a Martyr, that I may utterly destroi this tyraunt. Wyth
that the Abbot did weepe for gladnes, and much commended his fer-
vent zeale, as he tooke it. The Monke then beyng absolved of hys Abbot
for doing this act (aforehand) went secretely into a garden upon the
backe side, and finding there a most venemous Toade, so he pricked
him, and pressed him with his penknife: that he made him vomit all the
poyson that was wythin hym. Thys done, he conveyed it into a cuppe
of wyne, and with a smiling and flattering countenance, he sayd thus
to the kyng: If it shall lyke your princelye majesty, here is such a cup
of wyne, as ye never dronk a better before in all your lyfe tyme. I trust
this Wassall shall make all England glad. And with that he drak a great
draught thereof, the kyng pledging hym. The Monke anon after went
to the farmery, and there dyed (his guts gushing out of his belly) and
had continuallye from thenceforth three Monkes to sing Masses for hys
soul, confirmed by their generall chapter.

The monk gains absolution
from his abbot for what he
is about to do.

Right: 'The Monke tempereth his poyson into a Cup to give King John.'

Left: 'The Monke presenteth King John with his Cup of poyson beginning himself to the King.' (Note the toast 'Wassail my lige'.)

Right: 'The Monk dead of the poyson he drank to the King.'

Foxe continues on to explain that there are differing versions of John's death. Polidorus wrote that the king died of 'sorrow and heaviness of heart'. Radolphus Niger claimed that John had lost his life as a result of 'surfeting in the night'. Roger of Hoveden recorded that he died of a 'bloudy flixe', and Matthew Paris had him dying of 'heaviness of minde' which brought on a fever. This, in turn, John exacerbated by 'evil surfettyng & noughty diet, by eating Peaches and drinkyng of new Ciser, or as we call it Sidar'. Nevertheless, Foxe stays with the poisoning story as most writers 'agree in this that he was poysoned by the Monke above named'.

None of these versions appear to have come under contemporary challenge. This can only suggest that they were then part of the national understanding of the events that occurred around the death of the king. To all this must be added the local tradition, passed down many generations, which simply has it that King John was poisoned by a monk at Swineshead Abbey as a result of his earlier looting of the Cistercian abbeys at Crowland and Peterborough.

'King John ded of poyson.'

'A perpetual Masse sung daily in Swinsted for the Monk, that poysoned the King.'

It appears at least possible that a monk poisoned the king at a Cistercian abbey; the same Order that had suffered particularly under his tax regime, an Order that found its beginnings in the same source that started the Knights Templar. Both were probably involved in close co-operation with the building of the great cathedrals and other churches in a new, Middle Eastern style. The Cistercians, from the Abbot of Swineshead (Foxe's 'Swinestead') to the 'generall chapter' of the Order, clearly supported the murder, allowing Masses to be sung for the monk's soul. Also, the estate on which the abbey stood, and from which it received a considerable portion of its income, was owned by Robert de Gresley, the 5th Baron of Manchester. This was the same 'Roberto Gresley' who had signed the Magna Carta as one of the rebelling barons. Six months later, John had confiscated all de Gresley's land. At this, the baron made his way to Prince Louis (Foxe's 'Lodovicke') and gave homage to the invader.

The immediate outcome of the king's death was the appointment of a Knight Templar confrere to rule England.

9

WILLIAM MARSHAL – GUARDIAN OF THE GRAIL

One of the greatest lost stories of English history is that of Guillaume le Marechal – better known as William Marshal. He was born around 1146, the second son of John FitzGilbert, the Marshal of England (the same John that had been involved in bringing Becket to the Northampton trial in October 1164). The role of the Marshal was, initially, to look after the royal horses, but over time the Marshal began to take command in the army, eventually becoming its leader.

With an older brother ready to take over from the father, there was nothing for William to do but to be sent away as a trainee knight in the hope that he could make his own way in the world. He was, accordingly, sent to a cousin of his father, William de Tancarville, the hereditary Chamberlain of Normandy who made William his squire. It was the following year that, when riding in the service of his uncle, the Earl of Salisbury, who was guarding Eleanor of Aquitaine, an attempt was made to kidnap the queen. The earl was killed, Eleanor escaped, but William charged straight at the enemy, bowling them aside until he was unhorsed and brought down. Eleanor paid the ransom demanded for the young man and, two years later, he found himself, at the age of 24, as head of the 'mesnie', or military household, of the heir to the throne, Prince Henry. In 1173 William was knighted by William de Tancarville.

William had already become known for being tall, well-built and loyal. He soon began to obtain a reputation for utter fearlessness and awesome ability on the tournament field. To train his knights and, in due course, the prince himself, William would take them to the tournaments for battle experience. In the twelfth and thirteenth centuries, tournaments were quite different to the later form of regulated jousting in lists. The tournaments that William knew were full-blooded affairs, where large groups of knights attacked each other. There was little in the form of rules governing the event, and chivalry was something to be scorned. It was considered quite reasonable for a gang of knights to attack an individual or for a knight to seek out an opponent to settle a personal score. Once the opponent had been brought down, the victor (or victors) would be entitled to the defeated knight's horse, armour and weapons – and to demand a substantial bounty for the knight himself. Death and serious injury were not uncommon. It was just such an event for which William Marshal had been born. Wherever the fighting was at its hottest, there he could be found felling knights with his lance, sword and mace. In the meantime, he was also becoming very wealthy on the ransoms he was collecting from the fallen knights. From his time with the prince, he was never known to be beaten on the tournament field or in battle.

Matters took a serious turn when Henry II, listening to unfounded rumour, accused William of becoming too close to the prince's bride, Marguerite of France. William retaliated by demanding trial by combat with any knight – or knights – the king chose. Although the theory behind such events was supposed to be that God would choose the innocent over the guilty, the king refused to allow such combat to take place and the matter was quietly dropped.

On the death of Prince Henry (the 'Young King' as he had become known), William requested permission of Henry II to take the Cross and go on Crusade. This request was made in accordance with a promise he had made to the Young King – to take the Cross to the Church of the Holy Sepulchre on young Henry's behalf. With permission granted, he went to the Holy Land in the service of King Guy of Jerusalem – the same knight who had tried to kidnap Eleanor fifteen years earlier. However, for most of the time he was to be found fighting in company with the Knights Templar. These were men he could understand. Dedicated, single-minded, courageous and with a rigid faith, he found their company both inspiring and a pattern worthy of example. Nevertheless, William believed his path through life would be of greater benefit to his king and country if he served his sovereign directly.

William Marshal was not just supreme on the battlefield and the tournament, he was also highly intelligent with the skills of a diplomat. If he had killed the unarmoured Prince Richard during Henry II's retreat in 1188, it would have been seen as nothing more than an incident of war. Instead, he knew that the prospect of the Crown being passed on to the wholly unprepared and immature John would have been of no advantage to England whatsoever. On the other hand, after being given the responsibility for the Royal Treasuries by the dying Richard, William argued strongly and ensured that the Crown went to John rather than to Arthur in the belief that the son of the king had higher priorities than the grandson.

William Marshal had been promised the hand of Isabel de Clare, the daughter and sole heir of the Earl of Pembroke, by Henry, which was confirmed and approved after the king's death by Richard. The match brought great wealth and power to Marshal with lands in England, Ireland, Wales and on the Continent. Eventually confirmed as the Earl of Pembroke in his own right by King John, Marshal remained highly regarded

William Marshal unseats another opponent. (Matthew Paris illustration *c*.1250)

for his loyalty and courage. But trouble arose once again when Marshal paid homage to Phillip of France for his lands in Normandy. Although such arrangements were quite normal, John (despite having previously given permission for Marshal to pay the homage) took exception and deprived Marshal of much of his lands and took two of his sons as hostages. Five years later, with the outbreak of war against the Welsh, John summoned Marshal to help in the conflict. The earl responded loyally and such was his reputation that, at the signing of the Magna Carta, he was a witness alongside the Knights Templar Grand Master.

Marshal was an active supporter of religious orders and, amongst others, founded a Cistercian abbey on Bannow Bay, and a Cistercian priory at Duiske, both in Ireland. He was also a generous benefactor to the Knights Templar.

The death of King John in 1216 (with Marshal and the Master of the Temple amongst the executors of the king's will) meant that 9-year-old King Henry III would have to have someone to look after his and the country's interests. For the Council of Barons there could be only one man. William Marshal, Earl of Pembroke, and at one time a disregarded younger son, was appointed as Regent of England.

After the king had been crowned with a plain circlet of gold (due to the boy's small size), and with his regency confirmed by the Baron's Council, Marshal reissued the Magna Carta. This was a sound policy designed to bring most of the barons onto Marshal's side. With this achieved, he then had to drive the French from England.

By January 1217, a truce had been agreed and a large number of barons who had previously supported the French (including Marshal's own son, also named William) returned their loyalty to the king. Much of this change of allegiance was prompted by the successes of an obscure squire named William de Cassingham (probably modern-day Kensham in Kent). Known as Wilkin of the Weald, de Cassingham harried the French troops by land and sea to such an extent that the invaders were terrified of entering much of south-west England.

When the truce ended in April, Marshal decided to raise the siege of Lincoln Castle. The castle, still in the hands of Nicola de le Haye, remained under attack by rebel barons led by Gilbert de Gant and the Earls of Winchester and Hereford. Having failed to take the castle, de Gant was now supported by French troops commanded by the Comte de Perche. The French had brought up rock-throwing mangonels, and there was a grave risk that the castle would fall to the enemy, who now numbered 600 knights and 300 crossbow men.

Marshal mustered his forces at Newark – 400 knights, 250 crossbow men and several hundred foot soldiers – and then took them northwards to Torksey and on to Stow. They were escorted by many clergymen including Cardinal Gualo, the papal legate, and the Bishop of Winchester. At the old Saxon church at Stow, the papal legate excommunicated the besiegers whilst Marshal rallied and organised his forces. On the morning of 20 May they set off to march to Lincoln, some 8 miles away to the south-east.

At the head of the army, a Norman knight, Falkes de Breauté, led the crossbow men up the steep slopes of the Lincoln Edge to the old Roman road, Ermine Street, and advanced towards the city's north walls. There he found the old Roman gate, still beneath its original arch, only lightly defended but blocked with rubble. The front ranks of the crossbow men ran forward and began to pull down the barricade as their comrades' bolts drove the defenders back. Soon a gap was made wide enough for the crossbow men to enter the city, where they took to the roofs of houses and rained more bolts down upon the enemy. It was not long before the gate was cleared entirely, allowing Marshal to enter at the head of his knights. Once he had enough of them massed within the gate, with crossbow bolts hissing over their heads, Marshal, although now over 70 years old, led a charge towards the eastern gate of the castle. The French and their rebel baron allies were sent reeling back in disarray, before regrouping under de Perche in the area between the castle gate and the west front of the cathedral. Again Marshal charged with his knights and, according to the chronicler Roger of Wendover, 'sparks of fire were seen to dart, and the sounds of dreadful thunder were heard to burst forth from the blows of swords against helmeted heads'. With victory inevitable, Marshal called upon de Perche to surrender. The French leader, however, refused. At this, one of Marshal's knights spurred his horse and ran at de Perche with his sword. The tip of the weapon entered the eye-slit of de Perche's helmet and he fell to the ground, dead. The loss of their leader caused the French to flee from the city, running down the steep hill and pouring out of the south gate, pursued by Marshal's men.

Once the enemy had been put to flight, and the Lady Nicola, doughty defender of the castle, released from her besiegers, Marshal rode to Newark to inform the king of their victory. The job was not yet completed for the French still held London, and a French fleet was about to bring reinforcements

Effigy of William Marshal at the Temple, London.

to Prince Louis. But a convoy led by Hubert de Burgh (the same knight who had refused King John's demand to blind and mutilate Prince Arthur) routed the French, and Marshal's siege of London led to Louis seeking an end to the occupation of England. His price for the end of the conflict was 10,000 marks, which Marshal guaranteed from his own purse rather than extend the negotiations. In addition, the regent, with few exceptions, showed great magnanimity towards those English barons who had sided with the French.

With the exception of a few recalcitrant barons, who had to be brought to heel, Marshal concentrated on securing the country for the young king. At the beginning of May 1219, he became ill and, knowing that his end was near, retired to his home at Caversham, near Reading. Handing over the regency to de Burgh, Marshal took the habit of a Knight Templar in the days before his death on 14 May. Clothed as a Templar, he was buried in the London Temple, where his effigy may be seen today.

William Marshal was probably the greatest exemplar of knighthood ever to come from England. Uncompromising in his loyalty, steadfast in honour and gallant in character, he had served five kings with the greatest fidelity despite their personal flaws. Only in the case of King John is it possible that Marshal placed the country's interest over that of the king. If he had been involved in rescuing the Crown jewels and the royal relics from being sold off or falling to the French invaders, and if he had been aware of the murder of the king at Swineshead Abbey, it would have been for the benefit of the Crown, the country and for its people. It would be unthinkable that, having been closely involved with the royal family since Eleanor's time, he had not been aware of the gilded chalice, desperately sought by Becket and guarded by the Knights Templar. As a deeply committed Christian knight, and as a Templar confrere, William Marshal may well be considered as the original model of the Arthurian knight and as Guardian of the Grail.

10

THE HOLY BLOOD AND THE DOMINICANS

The death of William Marshal transferred the regency into the capable hands of Hubert de Burgh. The actual new regent was the new papal legate, Pandulf, but the day-to-day running of the country in the king's name was left to de Burgh. Like Marshal, de Burgh was a warrior knight of fearsome reputation whose defence of Dover Castle had played a major part in the removal of the French from England. He was also an accomplished courtier and diplomat who firmly believed that the King of England should be advised by Englishmen, and not by the large number of foreigners who had found important positions at court.

Chief amongst de Burgh's opponents were the Archbishop of Winchester, Peter des Roches, who had come from Poitiers in the service of Richard I, and his fellow Poitevin – and possible close relative – Peter de Rivaux, a highly influential friend of the king. De Burgh was not helped by Pandulf, who had a habit of interfering in every department of state and of bringing his relatives from Italy and putting them in positions of power in the English clergy.

Henry, now aged 13, was crowned for the second time in May 1220. The Pope had decided that the earlier coronation had not been properly carried out and demanded that it be repeated, this time at Westminster Abbey, with the Archbishop of Canterbury officiating. At this second coronation, the Crown jewels, supposedly lost in the Wash three and a half years earlier, were used, although the crown – or diadem – of St Edward that was placed on the head of the boy came from the relics of St Edward, which the Confessor had left in the care of the abbey.

The Archbishop of Canterbury, Stephen Langton, a supporter of de Burgh in his dislike of foreigners in positions of authority, went to visit the Pope and arranged for Pandulf to be removed from office. This, of course, meant that des Roches lost one of his most powerful allies in his campaign against de Burgh. Pandulf was appointed as Bishop of Norwich whilst des Roches was sent as archbishop of the Crusader church at Damietta – only to learn that his new responsibility had fallen to the Muslims. He returned to England in sullen determination to regain his former position close to the crown.

In April 1223 the Pope made a declaration that the 15½-year-old Henry was now old enough to rule in his own right. Fortunately for him, de Burgh, now no longer needed as regent, was appointed as justiciar, or chief justice, of the kingdom and remained by the king's side as his most respected advisor. This, in turn, infuriated des Roches who, in company with Falkes de Breauté (the same renegade Frenchman who led the attack at Lincoln), began to gather sympathetic barons around him. De Breauté, not a man with a great deal of finesse in matters of diplomacy, immediately ordered his brother, William, to kidnap a judge who had been making property decisions against him. William put his brother's order into immediate effect and, within days, the judge was in the dungeons of Bedford Castle.

The foolhardiness of the de Breauté brothers' action is clearly seen when it was realised that de Burgh happened to be mustering troops in readiness for an attempt to regain Poitiers for the Crown of England. Within three days of the judge's kidnap, Bedford Castle was under siege and Falkes de Breauté had fled to join the Earl of Chester who was in league with the rebellious Welsh prince Llewelyn. Expected to withhold a siege for at least a year, Bedford Castle surrendered within two months. The women were allowed to walk out unmolested, but the eighty prisoners taken, with the exception of three knights, were executed. The three who were spared were all Knights Templar.

With the fall of Bedford Castle and the flight of Falkes de Breauté, the foreign grip on the court of King Henry III was greatly weakened. Under de Burgh's direction, the posts at court went to Englishmen and it seemed that the kingdom was, at last, in the right hands and headed in the right direction. But then Henry came up hard against the problem that was to blight the remainder of his reign.

The struggle against the barons and against the Welsh had drained the Royal Treasury. There was some compensation in grabbing the 40,000 marks belonging to Falkes de Breauté, which had been entrusted to the Templars, but the financial problems were about to be compounded by the perceived need to mount an assault to regain Poitiers and to reinforce Gascony, the last English land on the Continent. As if that was not enough, the Pope decided to pursue another Crusade and demanded a large slice of the clerical and lay revenues to help pay for it. The Pope's demand was ignored, only to be replaced by a further demand from the king for funds to prosecute a war against the French.

An expedition was mounted in late 1229, but it had to be cancelled when too few ships arrived at Portsmouth to transport the troops. De Burgh was blamed by the king and, when the campaign was finally launched, it failed miserably. The king's Treasury was practically empty and many knights had to sell their horses and weapons just to survive. Again de Burgh was blamed. To add to his misery, the treaty negotiated with the French had involved Peter des Roches, now back on the scene. A campaign against the Welsh followed which saw the English defeated by poor logistics, apathy from the English barons and Welsh guerrilla tactics. De Burgh, who had led the campaign, now became the subject of the king's scorn, a view supported and encouraged by des Roches and other foreigners that clustered at Henry's court.

During the fighting against the Welsh, an English baron, William de Braose was captured and held by the Welsh prince Llewelyn. Unfortunately, whilst Llewelyn was away fighting, de Braose paid more than proper attention to the Welsh prince's wife, Joan – a half-sister to Henry. When he learned of this infidelity, Llewelyn hanged de Braose in front of 900 people. Astonished at the lack of response from the English, the Welsh leader mounted another assault on South Wales. When reports (which were almost certainly untrue) were made of churches full of women being burned down, Henry was forced to act. Despite the Pope excommunicating Llewelyn and placing an interdict on his lands, the response yet again failed to defeat the Welsh prince. Eventually a truce was agreed, and the excommunication and interdiction lifted. The failure of the campaign was laid firmly on de Burgh. The justiciar's chief ally, Archbishop Stephen Langton, had died in 1228 and the Pope – now Gregory IX – appointed the Chancellor of Lincoln, Richard le Grand (so named due to his unusual height) to the office. Le Grand immediately challenged de Burgh over the question of Tunbridge Castle which, the archbishop claimed, belonged to Canterbury. On failing to obtain his demands, le Grand went to the Pope with a list of complaints against de Burgh. It was to be le Grand's last act; having delivered his complaints, the archbishop died in Rome.

Gregory's response was to extract more taxes from the English clergy and, when his revenue collectors met resistance, to put yet more foreigners into the posts of the English bishoprics. So severe did this taxation become that one knight, Robert Twenge, operating under the *nom de guerre* of 'William Wither', organised gangs of men who attacked the Pope's taxmen and distributed the money amongst the poor. De Burgh, in full sympathy with the opposition to the papal demands, did nothing. This inaction by the chief justice of England outraged the Pope who sent letters to Henry demanding that action be taken against de Burgh. At this, de Burgh's most virulent enemy, Peter des Roches, joined in with the complaints against the justiciar.

Consequently, in late June 1232, the king dismissed de Burgh from office. The knight whom the chronicler Matthew Paris regarded as 'that most faithful Hubert who so often saved England from the devastation of the foreigners and restored England to England' was toppled in disgrace. The first thing the king did was to send for the Master of the Temple and demand that de Burgh's wealth, which had been deposited with the Templars, be handed over to him. Peter des Roches was back as the king's chief advisor and was made Earl of Gloucester. His close relative, Peter de Rivaux, was made sheriff of nineteen out of thirty-five counties and appointed as treasurer. To support their grip on power, des Roches authorised an influx of Breton and Poitevin mercenaries, and de Burgh ended up in prison.

As far back as 1220, Pandulf had placed the Treasury into the hands of the Knights Templar. The royal funds, however, had been ravaged by the failed French campaign and the Welsh disasters. The papal demands on the English clergy had reduced income from that section and the Jews – who only remained in England as a source of income for the king – had almost been drained of their wealth. Until the eventual arrival in England of Italian merchants, who began to open banking facilities in the country, the Templars were the only source of financial loans. At the beginning of his reign, Henry used the Templars as trustees of royal funds, as the middlemen in financial transactions and as a means of safe transfer of funds to the Pope and other sovereigns. But it was as a source of loans that the king mostly depended upon the Knights Templar. With almost certain inevitability, the more he came under debt to the Templars, the more his attitude to them began to change. In the beginning, for example, in 1225, the king referred to 'the king's beloved in Christ, the Master of the Knights of the Temple in England', but, as the debts mounted, so the relationship cooled. In 1248 the Master of the Knights Templar in England was fined 20 marks for keeping a rabbit warren. Two years later the king was extracting 100 marks from the Templars to renew their charters concerning their 'liberties', and in 1251 the king ordered the seizure of the Master's goods as security for an unpaid tax. In 1286, during the reign of Edward I, Henry's son, the Templars applied to 'appropriate' (have access to the fees of) the church of Donington, near Spalding in Lincolnshire, pleading poverty due to the 'immense expenses which the enemies of the Cross have brought upon this Order'.

A rebellion by Henry's barons against the Poitevins in 1234 had seen the expulsion of Peter des Roches and an increase of the king's burden of debt. Two years later, Henry married the 13-year-old Eleanor of Provence, the younger sister of the Queen of France. As her father, the Count of Provence, had spent all his revenues campaigning against his neighbours, Eleanor came without a dowry. Even worse, ignoring the lessons of Peter des Roches and the Poitevins, the new queen came with a number of Savoyard relatives who were soon rewarded with prominent positions, including one uncle who was made Earl of Richmond and another who was made Archbishop of Canterbury. They were quickly joined by several of the king's Lusignan half-brothers, one of whom was made Earl of Pembroke, and another, Bishop of Winchester. All were a drain on the king's purse and the cause of increasing annoyance amongst the English barons.

Henry's first targets for funds were the Jews. In 1250, for example, he demanded a total of 14,000 marks to be raised from all the Jews of England. Jews were also taxed individually. When Samuel Blund asked the king if he could be allowed to pay the same taxes as other Jews, the king agreed if it would be 'to the king's advantage' and charged Blund half a gold mark for the decision. Crimes between Jews were of no account unless bearing a monetary value. If it was proved that 'Cressus of Stamford, Jew, raped and abducted Eve Iudedecus from the Jewish school in the same city', his chattels were to be taken into custody until he paid 'one mark of gold to the king for that trespass'. If a Jew died, his debtors would have their debts transferred to the king. For Jews and their families, failure to settle the king's demands meant they were sent to prison and the only way to get out was to pay for their release.

Ironically, much of this money raised from the Jews was used to pay for the king's obsession with transforming Westminster Abbey into an English equivalent of the French king's glittering jewel of Sainte Chapelle, built by Louis IX to house two of the Christian world's greatest relics – a piece of the True Cross and the Crown of Thorns. Another way to help pay for the abbey's reconstruction was for Henry to demonstrate his Christian piety by increasing the number of relics the building would shelter. This, in turn, would attract more pilgrims, and more pilgrims meant more offerings.

To start with, the abbey already had a significant relic in the form of the remains of King Edward the Confessor, who had been made a saint in 1161. His remains were moved to the abbey in 1163 during a service led by Archbishop Thomas Becket. Other relics were also to be found in the great building. When founding the abbey, King Edward had presented the abbot with an arm of St Bartholomew and a similar limb of St Thomas the Apostle. Later, both were re-housed in jewelled reliquaries by Henry III. The abbey also housed the bones of the Holy Innocents (the children murdered on Herod's orders), and the stones used to kill St Stephen.

Henry himself presented the abbey with the head of St Maurice, a tooth of St Athanasius, an arm of St Sylvester, part of the head of St Christopher, unnamed parts of St Leonard, some clothing and a comb of St Thomas Becket, part of the Crown of Thorns and a stone bearing the footprint of Christ made as He ascended to Heaven.

Then, in 1247 came an astonishing surprise. The king received the Master of the Knights Templar in company with Masters John and Matthew, members of the retinue of the Patriarch of Jerusalem. They arrived bearing a very special gift from the Patriarch – nothing less than a crystal phial containing a portion of the Holy Blood. This wonderful relic, of value beyond comprehension, arrived with a letter from the Patriarch. In his communication, the Patriarch appealed for help from Henry to regain Jerusalem which, after a few years in Christian hands, had fallen first to the Khwarezmian Tartars and then to the Egyptian Arabs. Now in exile at Acre, the Patriarch went on to explain the recent history of the assaults upon his territory, particularly detailing the events at the sieges of Ascalon and Tiberias. In the midst of his narrative, he inserted a few lines, almost as an afterthought, explaining that the sample of the Holy Blood was entirely genuine ('and know most certainly and beyond doubt that this is truly that Blood which flowed from Christ's side') and had come from the treasures of the church in Jerusalem.

Henry was overjoyed. The Holy Blood far outweighed the piece of the True Cross and Crown of Thorns held in Sainte Chapelle. After all, they were only made holy by their contact with the Holy Blood, which was sacred in its own right.

Accordingly, Henry made great show of his new possession. Walking barefoot to the abbey beneath a covering held high by four spears, and wearing a simple cloak, Henry delivered the precious relic in person. The scene was recorded by the chronicler Matthew Paris:

> He carried it with both hands and although he came to rough or uneven sections of the road, he kept his eyes fixed always on either heaven or the phial. Two assistants supported his arms should his strength fail during his exertions. Bishops, abbots, and monks, numbering a hundred or more, tearfully singing and praising the Holy Spirit, went out to greet the king as he arrived ... Finally, he offered this rich and priceless gift, which had made all England illustrious, to God, to the church of St Peter at Westminster, to his beloved St Edward, and to the holy monks who minister there to God and His Saints.

But some aspects of the incident were extremely doubtful. Why, for example, were the Knights Templar involved? Furthermore, where did the relic come from?

The Templars may have been involved with nothing more than the simple transportation of the Holy Blood. They could have been employed to guard the relic as it journeyed from Acre, and the appearance of the Master of the Templars with the patriarchal envoys may have been just a question of ensuring its safe arrival. However, the Templars had in their possession a relic that the king would have been very keen to have seen in the reconstructed abbey. They held a gilded cup which was believed to have been used at the Last Supper and to have caught the blood of Christ on the Cross; a chalice that formed the foundation of a heroic myth that was still blossoming in literature. Unfortunately for the Templars, the relic had been given to their care by the king's grandmother. Consequently, Henry had a claim on the chalice that could not be ignored. There was only one way to avoid losing the relic, and that was to arrange for Henry to receive one of even greater importance. And it would not have been difficult to persuade the besieged Patriarch that it would be in his interest to provide something to distract the king from any attempts to obtain the chalice.

But where to obtain such a relic? It was true that throughout Christendom there were numerous relics of the Holy Blood, but many came from secondary sources such as the emperors at Constantinople or the treasures of Longinus at Mantua. Some were believed to have come from Jerusalem, but all centuries before the start of the Crusades. When Jerusalem was captured in 1099, there was no mention at the time of the discovery of the Holy Blood or any record of such a find in the succeeding years. This would be unusual in a city that was thronged with pilgrims who would have paid handsomely for a sight or to have been in the presence of such a precious relic. Nevertheless, the Patriarch managed to find some of the Holy Blood which was sent, unbidden, and uniquely to King Henry.

Centuries later, when the Holy Blood relic of Westminster Abbey was analysed, it was found to consist of 'honey coloured with saffron' (such a fraud was not at all uncommon. Even in the twentieth century, bones of the Virgin Mary held by the parish church of the Italian town of Calcata were proven to have come from a sheep – much to the delight of Pope Pius XII, who, in 1950, declared as dogma that Mary had ascended to heaven, bones and all).

There were soon to be plenty of new distractions to keep the king otherwise occupied. In 1238 Henry's sister, Eleanor

Above left: A Victorian impression of King Henry III.

Above right: A medieval reliquary chest showing the death of St Maurice.

of England, the widow of the son of William Marshal, married Simon de Montfort, a French knight who had a claim on his family property as Earl of Leicester. There was soon a disagreement between de Montfort and the king over the Frenchman's use of the king's name as a guarantor of a debt. After a period on Crusade, de Montfort rejoined Henry during the Poitou campaign. In 1248 de Montfort was sent as Seneschal to Gascony, the sole remaining English territory on the Continent, and succeeded in causing such discontent that the Gascons revolted against his rule. In 1253 Henry was forced to go to the region to settle the matter only to find Alphonso X, the King of Castile, about to resurrect an old claim to Gascony. To avoid an invasion, Henry resorted to the method most used by medieval royalty and arranged the marriage of his 14-year-old son, Edward, to Alphonso's 12-year-old half-sister, Eleanor. Despite such an unpromising beginning, the marriage of Edward (later to be known as 'Longshanks' from his height) and Eleanor was to prove happy and enduring.

In 1255 Henry consented to finance the Pope's war in Sicily when the Pope agreed that the king's second son, Edmund, would be made king of the island. But Henry was made to look foolish when he came close to being excommunicated for failing to raise the money needed. The appeal for funds also led to direct opposition from the English barons and to the Provisions of Oxford. These Provisions were drawn up by a twenty-four-man commission and placed the government of the country under the king advised by a fifteen-strong council of barons. Urged by the queen to stand his ground, by 1264, after first repudiating the Provisions, and then agreeing to them, the king found himself facing a barons' revolt led by de Montfort. The first clash took place at the battle of Lewis on 14 May and resulted in a defeat for the king and his capture, along with Prince Edward. Nevertheless, Edward escaped and met de Montfort in battle at Evesham in August. This time it was de Montfort who was defeated and much of his dismembered body scattered (his head was sent as a gift to the wife of one of the English barons). Three days after the battle, Henry issued a declaration stating that he was back in sole power.

The twenty years prior to the battle of Evesham had seen a fall in the reputation and status of the Knights Templar. They still held immense wealth, but many powerful people – not least the King of England – were in serious arrears to the knights; a situation uncomfortable to both parties. They were also under pressure on two other fronts.

In October 1244 the knights found themselves in a most unusual situation. At La Forbie (or Harbiyah), north-east of Gaza, they were facing an army consisting of Egyptians supported by Persian mercenaries, whilst alongside them fought Syrian Muslims and mounted Bedouin. At the end of the day, some 1,200 knights lay dead, including the Master and the Marshal of the Templars. Only thirty-three Templars survived.

Five years later, Louis IX landed at Damietta, at the mouth of the Nile, with 15,000 men and drove the Egyptians out. After consolidating their position, the Crusaders advanced up the Nile where the king's brother, Robert de Artois, scattered an Egyptian outpost guarding the town of Mansurah, the sultan's stronghold. De Artois, in complete disregard of his brother's orders, mounted a charge against the town. Massed to the rear of de Artois, the Knights Templar, not wishing to be seen as reluctant to become involved, joined in the charge. It was a fatal mistake, both for de Artois and the Templars. Once the knights reached the narrow streets and alleys, they were trapped and cut down by the Egyptians. Very few survived, and amongst the dead lay the king's brother.

With the fall of Antioch in 1268, only Tripoli and Acre remained in Christian hands, and several minds were beginning to enquire into the value of retaining the Knights Templar in a situation from which they could do little to regain Jerusalem and the Holy Sepulchre for Christianity. Certainly their mission to escort pilgrims had long disappeared.

In England, the Templars found themselves facing another, more insidious, threat. In 1216 a new Christian Order had been approved by the Pope. The Dominican Order, whose friars were dedicated to the saving of souls through preaching and the study of the Bible, found its origin in the Albigensian heresy. The Pope had ordered the Cistercians to organise missions amongst the Albigensians, but the monks made little headway. The reason for this was obvious to a visiting monk, the Castilian-born Dominic. Whilst the Cistercians were living in mild splendour, the heretics they were trying to convert back to Catholicism were, of their own choice, living a pure and simple life. Dominic decided to follow the example of the heretics and, dressing in simple clothes, possessing no property and living on alms, began to preach to the Albigensians. The success of his methods was startling, and soon many souls were rescued for the Catholic Church. This achievement led to the establishment of the Order and its support by the Pope, and soon convents of the Order spread throughout Europe.

In August 1221, within days of the death of Dominic (he was to be sanctified just over a decade later), Friar Gilbert de Freynet, Prior of the Order, led thirteen friars across the Channel to England. There he was met by Peter des Roches, the Bishop of Winchester, who led them to Canterbury, where they were welcomed by the archbishop. From there they made their way to Oxford where they founded a convent and a school. The Dominicans soon made their mark with their pious conduct, their scholarship and their preaching. They chose to work in the towns and cities amongst the sick and the poor. There was plenty for them to do, for the parochial clergy had little time for their congregations other than as a source of tithes. Preaching by the parish priest was almost unheard of, and although the bishops frequently invited the friars to preach in their presence, the local clergy viewed the black-cloaked 'Blackfriars' with hostility.

It was not just among the poor that the Dominicans made their influence felt. The great Dominican scholar Roger Bacon frequently preached at the royal court, and in 1256 the king chose the Dominican Prior John de Darlington to be his confessor. Perhaps the most telling incident was the appointment of de Darlington as one of the twenty-four commissioners who produced the Provisions of Oxford in 1258 – an appointment that would normally have gone to the Master of the Templars. The king gave land and funding to the Dominicans, as did his wife and his daughter-in-law, Eleanor of Castile, and in 1272 the senior Dominican in England, Friar Robert Kilwardby, was appointed as Archbishop of Canterbury.

11

THE FINAL GUARDIAN

Prince Edward had taken the Cross in 1268 with the intention of joining the French king, Louis IX, on Crusade. As usual, the greatest difficulty was the raising of funds for the expedition, and the money was only obtained with the help of a loan of over £17,000 from Louis. Edward left England in August, accompanied by his wife Eleanor, who was determined to go on Crusade with him. They had originally intended to go to the aid of Acre, the last Christian stronghold in the Holy Land, which was under siege by the Muslims. Instead, they learned that Louis had gone to Tunis to try and secure a base on the coast of North Africa. However, the French had been struck by the plague. Louis had contracted the disease and died. This resulted in the French deciding to return home, but Edward continued to Acre.

The arrival of the English forces made little difference to the beleaguered city. A few raids against the Muslims were organised, but little was achieved. An appeal for help to the Mongols massing in the north brought about some relief when Aleppo was raided, but when the King of Cyprus signed a ten-year truce with the Muslims, any hopes of regaining Jerusalem, or even of a successful defence of Acre, disappeared.

Whilst preparing to leave, Edward suddenly found himself faced with a Muslim assassin. The prince fought the enemy off and managed to kill him, but not before he, during the struggle, had been stabbed with a poisoned dagger. It was to be several months before Edward fully recovered from the attack and, when he did, he learned that his father had died and he had become the new King of England.

Henry III had died in November 1272. At the end, exhausted and in debt, the king could hardly look back on a successful reign. Continually provoked over papal and secular tax-raising, with a miserable failure and loss of stature on the question of the Sicilian kingdom, and his disappointing warfare against the Poitevins and the Welsh, he was forced to face his own barons on the field of battle, themselves provoked in part by his queen's aggressive policy of promoting her own relatives and other foreigners.

Matters did not look too good either for his son, the tall Edward 'Longshanks'. On the day of his coronation, at which Archbishop Robert Kilwardby officiated, Edward had a personal debt to the Knights Templar of over £28,000. He could ignore any amount he owed to the Jews, but he could not disregard the enormous debt he owed to Italian merchant bankers, a relatively new breed of entrepreneur who found England an easy place to conduct new business, despite the fact that he charged them 6,000 marks a year to do so. To make matters even more awkward, Edward used the facilities of the Templars to repay his debts to the Italians.

The debt to the Templars is unlikely to have included the treasure taken by Edward in an incident that happened in June 1263. On that day, the prince arrived in London with an armed force. His father had been forced to take shelter in the Tower of London and his mother had been pelted with stones and spat at by the Londoners, who had turned out in support of the rebellious barons. Looking for a source from which he could pay his men, Edward's eye fell instantly upon the New Temple, the great treasury of the Knights Templar.

Accompanied by Robert de Waleran, Chancellor of England and Warden of the Cinque Ports, Edward burst into the building and demanded that his mother's jewels be produced. Any objections were brushed aside and when access had been gained to the vaults, the prince ransacked the treasury of jewels, cash and precious articles to the value of £10,000.

It is extremely unlikely that a particular silver-gilt chalice was removed, for the prince would not wish to arouse the anger of the Church over the theft or mismanagement of a precious relic. As for his mother's annoyance at the loss of her jewels, she was, no doubt, soon mollified by the massive award of 20,000 marks raised by de Waleran by fining the citizens of London for being on the wrong side during the Barons' War.

In 1270, on the death of the Archbishop of Canterbury, Boniface of Savoy, Prince Edward tried to have one of his friends, Robert Burnell, appointed to the post. In this he was challenged by the Chapter at Canterbury who wanted the Prior of Christ Church Priory, William Chillenden, appointed. The Pope, Gregory X, rejected Burnell, possibly on the grounds that he had maintained a mistress for many years and was rumoured to have several sons. The way seemed clear for Chillenden and moves were made towards his appointment, only to have the Pope, almost certainly on the advice of Petrus Tarentasia, his intimate friend and a Dominican friar, appoint Robert Kilwardby – the senior Dominican in England.

Kilwardby was a theological scholar and philosopher of distinction, but it was probably not for his academic skills that he was manoeuvred into the post of Archbishop of Canterbury. When he took over the role, he found, thanks to the work of Boniface, that the archbishopric was free of debt. Despite showing little interest in the business of State, and apparently restricting himself to spiritual matters, Kilwardby soon began to run up considerable debts and, by 1278, the See of Canterbury was as much in debt as it had ever been. The archbishop lost his papal support when Gregory X died in 1276. Gregory's successors, Adrian V and John XXI, only had months in office. As a result, Kilwardby found himself under the papal direction of Pope Nicholas III, a firm friend of the Franciscans – mendicants who, whilst not directly opposed to the Dominicans, looked with unease upon their fellow friars.

In March 1278 the Pope made a surprising decision. He removed Kilwardby from the office of Archbishop of Canterbury and promoted him as Cardinal Bishop of Porto and Santa Rufina. When he left England, Kilwardby took with him all the administrative records of Canterbury – none of which were ever seen again. Within eighteen months, the former archbishop was dead and his place at Canterbury taken by King Edward's first choice for the office, Robert Burnell.

It is not too fanciful to see in Kilwardby's behaviour an echo of a former Archbishop of Canterbury. His wanton extravagance at a time when the king's finances were under strain, his reluctance to fulfil his state duties and his theft and probable destruction of the Canterbury records, suggest the behaviour of someone frustrated in ambition. Was he trying, and failing, to obtain a gilded cup for the cathedral at Canterbury?

No evidence remains of the next stage of the chalice's journey. How it arrived in its final hands is not known and must remain no more than speculation, but one reasonable route is open to suggestion, one that may come close to the real path.

By 1278, Edward was in a desperate situation regarding his finances. Another war against the Welsh had brought little reward and had proved another severe drain on the Treasury. There remained, however, one way to raise funds, and that was to sell one or more of the relics held either by the Templars on the king's behalf or in his own Treasury. Chief among the relics was the chalice used by Christ at the Last Supper and by Joseph of Arimathea to catch His blood as He died upon the Cross.

The trade in relics was nothing unusual. In 1236 the Emperor of Constantinople, Baldwin II, had pawned the Holy Crown of Thorns to Venetian merchants. Unable to redeem his pledge, Louis IX settled the loan and brought the relic to Paris. Five years later, Louis purchased fragments of the True Cross and the tip of the Holy Lance from Templars based in Syria. As recently as 1270, a phial of Christ's blood was purchased from the Count of Flanders and presented to Hailes Abbey, a Cistercian house founded in Gloucestershire and consecrated in 1251 (the blood later turned out to be from a duck). Nevertheless, despite the acknowledged trade in relics, the Knights Templar, and others who knew of the existence and provenance of the chalice, would have been most reluctant to have the treasured possession placed on the open market.

The king, probably aware of the Templars' reluctance, then increased the pressure on both them and the Church. For centuries, it had been the custom of people from all walks of life to donate land to both organisations, either as a gift or upon death. As a result they had become the owners of vast amounts of property. That in itself was not a particularly pressing problem, but the result of such transactions affected the income of the king, his earls and other lords and barons. Under normal circumstances, the possession of land carried with it certain responsibilities to the overlord such as service in war or the payment of taxes. If the land passed into the hands of the Church or the Templars, the overlords were placed at an immediate disadvantage as neither organisation owed service or paid taxes, nor would either the Church or the Templars – as perpetual corporations – die and leave the land to a successor. The result was a drying up of income and service which, in the end, could affect the defence of the realm.

As it was, laws against this 'mortmain' (from the 'dead hand' that controlled the outcome) had existed since the creation of the Magna Carta, but the king was allowed to issue licences for the law to be bypassed. Henry III, being a friend of the Church, rarely hesitated to allow such permits. Edward and his lords, on the other hand, were determined to be less charitable. In 1279 the 'Statutes of Mortmain' were enacted. No more land was to pass into the hands of the Church or the Templars.

At this point, the Templars were on uncertain ground. Their role as the shock troops of the Church had all but faded away, and their banking infrastructure had contracted in the face of Italian competition. Cracks in their much-vaunted security had also been exposed by the raid on their vaults by the king just sixteen years earlier. The time may have arrived to seek compromises.

Certainly the king was prepared to compromise. Although the Statutes of Mortmain appeared to be watertight, there remained one tiny loophole. Land could be transferred through a system of trusteeships which circumvented the statutes. The overlord would still be able to demand the return of the land if the original owner died, but the legal procedures required could render the effort and costs involved pointless. Nevertheless, the loophole could be closed by the king with just a stroke of the pen. This regal compromise could, and might have been, matched by the Templars through their cancelling of the debts owed to them by the king.

If that was the case, what then of the chalice? Although saved in the short term from being offered for sale, the Templar security could now no longer be guaranteed. Nor could the Knights Templar, owing loyalty solely to the Pope, be entirely trusted not to send it to Rome, or even to sell it themselves to recoup the losses in cancelling the king's debt. In addition, the Grand Master was distantly related to the King of France, who would be extremely keen to add the cup to his collection of passion relics housed in the Sainte Chapelle.

There was only one answer. A new custodian or guardian would have to be found – one who was agreeable to the king, to the Templars and to the Church.

Giving the Grail to the Archbishop of Canterbury, a Franciscan, was out of the question. His close ties with the Pope – who was also a Franciscan – would render the relic's security at equally grave risk. The Archbishop of York, Walter Giffard, was too close to the king – his parents had been the king's guardians. Furthermore, Giffard had run up considerable debts whilst in office. The bishop of the largest diocese in England was the Bishop of Lincoln, but Richard de Gravesend had supported Simon de Montfort against the king's father and had been suspended from office and exiled for two years. But de Gravesend demonstrated one important redeeming factor – he died in December 1279, leaving the way open for a man who did fit the requirements of Guardian of the Grail.

In 1279 Oliver Sutton was the Dean of Lincoln Cathedral. His family came from the Nottinghamshire village of Sutton-on-Trent. On his mother's side he was modestly well connected with one uncle, Henry de Lexington, having been Bishop of Lincoln between 1254 and 1257. Two other uncles held high office under the Crown, one as a justice in the Court of Common Pleas, another as chancellor and steward of the Household of Henry III. Yet another uncle, Stephen, became the Abbot of Clairvaux Abbey – the position previously held by the Cistercian St Bernard.

Having served as the Rector of Shelford in Cambridge, Sutton studied canon and civil law at Oxford and was made a Canon of Lincoln in 1270. He had intended to remain at his academic studies, but in 1275 he left Oxford on being appointed Dean of Lincoln.

As the two previous bishops had been appointed from the post of dean, there was no difficulty in finding precedents for Sutton's appointment as bishop. There was also the possible question of the king's approval of Sutton's advancement, backed by the Knights Templar. The latter support may have contained more than just an agreement of the king's choice.

The Templars' battle-shield consisted of a white field below a 'chief sable' (wide black bar across the top). Sutton's shield as bishop had a white field with a 'canton sable' (a black bar extending from the top left-hand corner, or facing, of the shield to a third or halfway across the top). His election to bishop was 'by way of inspiration'; in other words, immediate and unanimous.

Sutton was consecrated by the Archbishop of Canterbury at Lambeth Palace on 19 May 1280 and enthroned at Lincoln on 8 September. The timing was immaculate. Just under a month later, Sutton was to play a leading part in what was certainly the biggest event to occur in Lincoln before or since.

Hugh of Avalon had begun his religious life as a Carthusian monk. Brought to England in 1179 by Henry II as Prior of Witham Priory in Somerset, he made such an impression that he was elected as Bishop of Lincoln seven years later. The cathedral had been badly damaged by an earthquake the previous year and the new bishop took a leading role in its rebuilding. Although considered a friend of the king, Hugh did not hesitate in blocking attempts to obtain posts in his diocese for the king's nomination, but he always tempered his opposition with diplomacy. The bishop was extraordinarily active in the management of his diocese. Whenever possible, he chose to live at his Lincolnshire residences and constantly

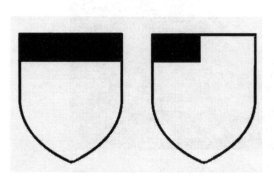

The Templars' battle-shield (*left*) and Bishop Oliver Sutton's shield (*right*).

Bishop (later 'Saint') Hugh of Avalon with his swan companion.

carried out visitations of his bishopric, at the same time presiding over the construction of the cathedral.

Hugh was known for his defence of the Jews, and when, at the start of King Richard's reign, a wave of anti-Semitism swept the country, the bishop did all he could to prevent attacks upon them. He was also known for his strict moral code, straightforwardness and his refusal to bow to greater authority when he believed that a wrong would result. On one occasion he even had the temerity to physically shake King Richard, who was so surprised that he broke into laughter and accepted the bishop's point of view. The bishop also had the rare honour of being adopted by a swan. The bishop and the bird had met at his Stowe residence and the swan followed him wherever he went, even sleeping by his bed. Many subsequent images of Bishop Hugh show him in company with the swan. Such an impression did Hugh make that, on his death in 1200, his coffin was carried by King John, King

St Hugh is borne
to his burial by
kings and bishops.
A drawing of a
panel in the rose
window of Lincoln
Cathedral known as
the 'Dean's Eye'.

William of Scotland, archbishops and bishops, in the presence
of a huge throng of more bishops, abbots and priors.

Twenty years after his death, Bishop Hugh was canonised by
Pope Honorius III and, in 1280, it was decided to 'translate' (i.e.
move) his remains to the half-completed eastern extension of
the cathedral, known as the Angel Choir and the Chapel of St
John the Baptist. The translation was to take place in the presence
of the king and his queen, Eleanor of Castile; the king's brother,
Edmund Plantagenet, Earl of Leicester, and his wife, Blanche
d'Artois, the dowager Queen of Navarre; the Earls of Gloucester,
Lincoln and Warwick; the Archbishops of Canterbury and
Edessa; the Bishops of Lincoln, Bath, Ely, Norwich, Worcester,
Llandaff and St Asaph; the Bishop-Elect of Exeter; and 230
knights. The whole event was to be paid for by Thomas Bek, the
brother of the Bishop of Durham, who was to be consecrated
Bishop of St David's as part of the translation celebrations.

The Archbishop of Canterbury, Bishop Sutton, the king and
the queen, lifted the body of the saint from its 80-year-old
coffin. As they did so, the head became detached. Beneath
the body lay a pool of sacred oil which was reverently collected. The head was placed on a silver platter as more oil
poured from the mouth – a sure sign of sanctity. The body was
placed in a gold- and silver-lined shrine in the centre of the
Angel Choir between the high altar and the altar dedicated to
St John the Baptist. The head was placed in a jewelled casket
which, in turn, was secured to its own shrine to the north
of St John the Baptist's Chapel.

The event proved to be a great success and, no doubt, the
king would wish to reward those involved. It is entirely possible that the king presented a silver-gilt chalice to Bishop
Sutton in gratitude for the work he had done. The giving of
cups in various forms was commonplace and has lasted into
the twenty-first century in the shape of trophies for sport-
ing and academic success. Queen Eleanor of Aquitaine had

presented a jewelled gold cup to the abbey at St Albans; Abbot Symon of the same abbey presented his church with a 'very large cup of gold adorned with foliages and flowers of the most delicate workmanship'. When King John of France was taken prisoner after the battle of Poitiers in 1356, he exchanged gold cups with Edward III on his release. In his will, Richard II left a gold cup to every Christian monarch and James I gave the Spanish Ambassador a gold cup that had once been a gift to Charles VI of France in the fourteenth century.

It is possible that Sutton did not know what had been put into his charge and that it had not been explained to him that he was now the Guardian of the Grail. There would, no doubt, have been considerable temptation to display the chalice as a relic, but the Templars would certainly not have agreed. To advertise the fact that they had been persuaded to release the artefact would not have been welcome. Nor would the king want the fact broadcast that he had obtained relief from his debt through threatening to sell the chalice. As for Sutton, he could have used the relic as his Communion cup without compunction for, at that time, only the priest officiating at the Communion used the vessel.

The only obvious problem lay in the fact that, as a royal gift, the chalice was of rather poor quality. Silver-gilt rather than gold, it was plain to any observer that it was not of the best manufacture, particularly with its rather crude riveting on the stem. Entirely undecorated, it even fell behind the generally basic design of Bishop Remigious' chalice which, at least, had the merit of lines scored around its bowl and at the junction of bowl and stem. That belonging to Sutton's predecessor, de Gravesend, bore a modest decoration and gilding, whereas Bishop Grosseteste's chalice was a fine example of the silver-smith's art. Perhaps the reason given for the low quality of Sutton's 'gift' was shortage of funds on the sovereign's part.

Bishop Sutton proved to be a gifted administrator. He worked hard on his diocesan duties and was known for his strict application of both canon and civil law, yet, wherever he could, he tempered his judgements with common sense. On one occasion, noted in his records:

> Richard of Crowland appeared before Bishop Sutton at the Old Temple, London, for confirmation of his election as abbot of Crowland in succession to Ralph. The Bishop declared the election invalid on grounds of incorrect procedure, and deprived the electors of their power to choose an abbot on this occasion. He then appointed the said Richard as abbot upon his own responsibility, November 5, 1280, and consecrated him at Theydon, November 10, 1280.

On another occasion he wrote to a somewhat less than thorough abbot:

> To the Abbot of Bec, greeting, and the hope that, for the love of justice, he may care for the rights of others as he does for his own. God knows that we do not write these things to you in the arrogance of presumption, but in order that by this example, you may know how easily and quickly you may bar the way to complaints.

He then went on to show the abbot how to submit a letter of presentation to a bishop.

Sutton even challenged the king when Edward demanded an extra tax from the clergy. In concert with the Archbishop of Canterbury, Robert Winchelsey, Sutton refused to pay the tax. However, the Archbishop of York gave in and paid one-fifth of the church's revenues to the king. At this, the king insisted that all clergy do the same. Only Winchelsey and Sutton stood firm and both had their personal property confiscated. Behind Sutton's back, his friends made a deal with the Sheriff of Lincoln that the officer should extract a fifth of the value of Sutton's goods to settle the matter. Winchelsey and the king were reconciled the following year.

Communion plate and part of a crosier found in the tomb of Bishop Remigious, the eleventh-century founder of Lincoln Cathedral.

Sutton also proved to be a builder. He ordered the construction of the cathedral cloisters and contributed 50 marks to the expenses. He also began the work of building the Vicar's Court to house some of the cathedral staff. When the cathedral was first erected by Bishop Remigious, the church of St Mary Magdalen had been destroyed. Consequently, ever since the loss of their parish church, the parishioners had held their services in the cathedral nave. Sutton ordered the building of a new church dedicated to the same saint close by the cathedral.

The bishop's biggest building effort started in 1285, when he applied to the king for permission to have a substantial, castellated wall built around the cathedral close, giving as his reason the protection of the clergy as they attended late-night services:

> for their better safety from night attacks in passing from their houses to the said church, to enclose the precincts of the said church with a wall, 12 feet high, in suitable places, at Pottergate Street and at the street leading from the high road of the bailey to the Eastgate with the two adjoining lanes on the north side: the said wall to be provided with sufficient gates with locks, to the custody of which they had, their successors shall appoint one of their body to close them at dusk and open them again before sunrise.

The king granted permission, although whether for the reasons given or for the protection of a precious item now held within the cathedral is not known.

At the chapel (probably the parish church close by the palace) at Nettleham, just outside the city, on the evening of St Brice's Day, 13 November 1299, Sutton, now of 'a great and good old age', was kneeling at prayer whilst his priests and clerks were singing matins. They had just begun the first verse of the hymn *Iste Confessor Domini Sacratus*:

> He, whose confession God of old accepted,
> Whom through all ages all now hold in honour,
> Gaining his guerdon this day came to enter
> Heaven's high portal.

Before they had completed the verse, Bishop Oliver Sutton, Guardian of the Grail, 'rendered up his spirit to his Creator'. Eight days after his death, the canons of Lincoln Cathedral rode out to escort his body back to the cathedral. It was carried by his friends and relatives and a cross was erected where the procession rested in the middle of the journey. At the city gates, the bier was handed over to the mayor, sheriff and other leading citizens, who carried it into the great church.

Unusually for a bishop, who were normally interred in above-ground chest tombs, Bishop Sutton's grave was dug between the first two columns from the eastern end of the church on the north side of the uncompleted Angel Choir. Before the lead sheets surrounding the body were soldered, a gilt chalice, a paten and his crosier were placed alongside the bishop.

At some later stage, possibly as the work on the Angel Choir was drawing to a close, someone, either with a sense of fun or with a darker purpose, carved a 12in-high minor devil – or imp – and placed it high above a column in the Choir at the point where the column divides to form the arches on either side.

The column chosen for this particular decoration is the one at the foot of Bishop Sutton's grave. The cloven-hoofed imp was carved in a seated posture with its right leg across its left knee. The creature has a full head of hair, bushy eyebrows and a gap in the upper front teeth that seem all too human. From the head rise a pair of horns which, curiously, have had their sharp tips removed (it may be fanciful to note that a cup made of animal horn was referred to in old French as a 'graal'). In front of and below the horns, a pair of cow-like ears project horizontally. The upper body seems to be hairy, whilst a circle around the left ankle suggests that the imp is wearing some sort of hose. The imp's 'hands' rest on the right leg, each hand consisting of three fingers, which all end in a sharp claw. If the horns and ears were removed, the head, with its monkish fringe, thick eyebrows and gap teeth, could be taken for a caricature of a real person – a practice not unknown in church stonemasonry. Of especial interest, however, is the fact that the imp is seated, giving rise to the possible Middle English word for 'sat' which is 'sitton' – the word being a possible pun for 'Satan', or more probably, 'Sutton'. Is the Lincoln Imp a carved reference to the grave below?

As if that was not enough to suggest a link with Bishop Sutton, there remains yet another clue. It may be entirely coincidental, but it is worthy of consideration. Just below the ankle of the raised right leg there appears to be something in the shape of an arrowhead – or pointer – just below the imp's left knee. It is just possible that this feature is intended to represent the lead end of a belt, where it has been so shaped to facilitate entry into a buckle. If, however, it is considered as a pointer, the next thing to consider is the lower left leg itself. The lower leg does not stand vertically, but is angled (from the viewer's point of view) slightly from the right – at the knee – to the left at the hoof. If the direction indicated by the pointer is followed down the leg and extended beyond the hoof, the line ends up at Sutton's grave.

The Lincoln Imp. Note the pointer and the angled lower left leg.

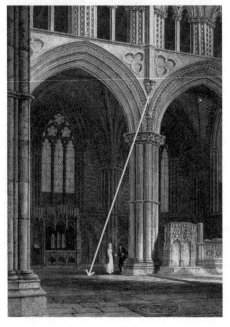

The angle of the Imp's left leg points out the site of the Grail.

There may be yet even more evidence to link Bishop Sutton and the Lincoln Imp. Archaeological studies of the bishop's palace at Nettleham have failed to reveal any sign of a private chapel for the bishop, and subsequent architectural plans of the site do not show such a chapel. The reason for this could be that the church at Nettleham, originally Saxon, but redesigned in the Early English style at the time of Bishop Sutton, was just a few paces from the palace. This church could be the chapel in which the bishop worshipped and died.

Inside the church at Nettleham, the northern aisle is separated from the nave by an arcade of arches supported on stout piers. The capitals of the piers are decorated with stylised acanthus leaves, other examples of which can be found in the cathedral, suggesting that the same sculptors were responsible for both. The wall area at the top of the piers, between where the arches rise and separate (the spandrel), is ornamented with the fading remains of late thirteenth-century paintings, mainly of flowing, possibly floral, patterns, topped in parts by a chequer-board design. The arches incorporate plain 'labels' – carved strips of masonry that follow the curve of the arch. Sometimes these end at the tops of the piers; others are decorated before they reach the pier tops with a single sculpture of acanthus leaves.

One of the pier capitals has an interesting addition; the head of a man has been carved (or inserted) at the point where the labels of the flanking arches meet the capital, i.e. at the base of the spandrel. The carving, which has survived the centuries to remain in a good condition, shows the face of a wide-eyed, tight-lipped man, with an unmistakable monkish fringe along the top of his forehead. On top of the man's head rests a solid-looking block of stone showing two sides of a rounded square. Immediately above the carved head and its surmounting block, and placed in a most ungainly, inelegant position, is a carving of acanthus leaves. The whole arrangement is unsatisfactory to the eye, lacks symmetry and gives rise to the possibility that the acanthus leaves were later so placed to prevent anything being put on top of the block above the head.

The church's printed history declares that the head, with its surmounting block, is likely to be a Master Mason, wearing a 'mason's cap'. The 'cap', however, is not so much worn as simply resting on top of the man's head. In this case, it is more likely to be a corbel to hold something such as a small statue or image, or a sconce intended to hold a candlestick. If it is the latter, why should a candle be required in such a position? What would it illuminate? The answer, undoubtedly, is that in the lower part of the spandrel, in a similar place to the Lincoln Imp, is a painted imp. The head is similar to the Lincoln Imp, although, if there had ever been a detailed body attached, it has long since disappeared. Is this another indicator of the link between the bishop and the Lincoln Imp? Was the clumsy addition of the acanthus leaves a deliberate means of preventing a candle from being lit to illuminate the image above? Why not remove the sculpted head or paint over the image? Whatever the reason, there is a possibility that at both the probable scene of Sutton's death and at the place of his burial, at about the same time, an imp has been depicted in a spandrel close by.

A caricature of Bishop Sutton?

Another odd, and possibly unaccountable aspect of the chalice in Bishop Sutton's tomb being the Holy Grail, is to be found in yet another link to the Arthurian myth. When the wounded and dying Arthur is taken from the battlefield at Camlann, he is put on board a boat sailed by three queens (actually, the three Norns, or 'Fates', Urdr, Verdandi and Skuld, of Norse mythology). They escort the king to Avalon, a mysterious island where Arthur will remain until called to come to England's defence in some far-off future.

In 1280 Edward I, King of England, came to the relocation of the body and head of St Hugh, the Bishop of Lincoln between 1186 and 1200. St Hugh had been born in the Chateau of Avalon, a small village in the south-east of France, and was widely known as 'Hugh of Avalon'. It would not be unreasonable to ask what the odds are in favour of a King of England going to 'Avalon' – in this case a person, rather than a place – whilst bearing a gilded chalice, and that chalice being the Holy Grail. No clear link remains, but the possibility of an unknown path leading to St Hugh cannot be ignored.

Even beyond the precincts of the cathedral, there may be another clue to the site of the Holy Grail. Certainly from the fourteenth century, and possibly from its earliest decade, the city of Lincoln has had a coat of arms. As if a signpost down the centuries, the coat of arms consists of a white shield bearing a red cross, exactly in the manner of a Templar shield. In the centre of the cross is a gold fleur-de-lys, the symbol of the Virgin Mary – the patron saint of the cathedral. Together, the two symbols seem to be a heraldic version of 'X marks the spot'.

There remains one further aspect of the chalice which needs to be addressed. Many would agree with Rosalind M.T. Hall, the editor of Bishop Sutton's registers and rolls, that the chalice placed in the bishop's grave was 'a fine example of thirteenth century workmanship'. If true, then that chalice is unlikely to have been the Holy Grail used by Christ twelve centuries earlier. However, the editor's statement is true only in so far that there were many chalices of that pattern in use in the thirteenth century. It does not preclude a cup of the same design being in use centuries earlier. This is clearly shown by the image on silver and bronze Jewish coins minted in Jerusalem between AD 66 and AD 68 – about three decades after the death of Christ. On them can clearly be seen an image of a chalice of almost exactly the same design as the one in Bishop Sutton's grave. The only difference is that the chalice depicted on one of the coins appears to have a beaded rim. This decoration suggests that the plain chalice brought from the Holy Land by Eleanor of Aquitaine, which ended up being buried alongside the bishop, was a perfectly ordinary vessel of the type that would have been used in the house of the man hosting the Last Supper – and which was later used to catch the blood of Christ as He hung on the Cross. This then became the Holy Grail, the only object to have come down to us through the centuries which has a direct connection with Christ.

Examples of Jewish coins minted in Jerusalem between AD 66–68. All show variations of a chalice.

EPILOGUE

For almost 600 years, the gilded chalice stood upright on its base in the empty silence of the tomb, whilst just a few feet above the world went about its business. The Knights Templar, the original Guardians of the Grail, fell to the greed of Phillip the Fair in 1307. History tells us that he found nothing in the Paris Temple, but not what he was actually looking for. It has always been assumed that he was merely looking for random treasure, but he may, after reaching a height of religious fervour following the death of his wife, have been looking for something much more specific that might have been transferred to the Paris Temple (after all, at one time the English Crown jewels had been put there). The hope of adding a particular gilded chalice to the collection of relics held in Sainte Chapelle would – for Phillip at least – have been a powerful incentive. When nothing was found, Phillip handed the Templars over to Dominican inquisitors (who were known by the pun '*Domini canes*' – 'Dogs of God') to face a ragbag of absurd charges.

Probably the most outrageous accusation against the Templars in medieval eyes was the charge of spitting on the Cross, which may have had more depth to it than is accorded by many historians. Most studies refer to the captured Templars who had been beheaded or flayed alive by the Muslims after the fall of the castle at Safed. The knights had refused to save their lives by publicly denying Christ. How, they argue, could such men admit to defiling the Cross? The problem here is that denying Christ is quite different from despising the instrument of execution on which He died. The Cross, as a symbol of Christianity, did not appear until three centuries after the death of Christ, and had already been used frequently amongst earlier religions. One suggestion for its origin as a Christian symbol is that the Emperor Constantine introduced the Cross as a means of bringing together pagan and Christian elements in his army. The pagans recognised the Cross as a symbol of the sun god, and the Christians accepted it as an emblem of Christ's sacrifice. A Christian order of warrior monks may well have taken the view that the timbers to which Christ was nailed were not worthy of adoration, only of contempt and hatred. There could have been no better test of obedience for a medieval knight, brought up to worship the Cross, than to find himself being required to defile it during his initiation. The red cross on his tunic and mantle, on the other hand, were not symbols representing an instrument of torture, but the sign of a martyr. It is worth pointing out that the churches and cathedrals the Templars funded – for example, Chartres – were built without a single representation of the Cross. The view that the Cross was an inappropriate symbol for Christians would not have been unique to the Templars. From the earliest Christians (who used the symbol of a fish) to modern Christian sects, the Cross is rejected. Along with the other accusations, the charge of spitting on the Cross was widely admitted by the French Templars, but little reliance can be placed on such admissions as they were obtained under unendurable duress. In England, however, where torture was not used, three knights admitted to the charge.

In England, Edward I had died earlier that year (1307) and his son, Edward II, showed no interest in harrying the Templars in the hope of discovering a relic. The following year, the Pope, Clement V, absolved the Templars from all the charges against them, yet, in 1312, under pressure from the French king, he abolished the Order. Within a year, both the Pope and the king were dead.

Around the year 1470, Sir Thomas Malory wrote *Le Morte d'Arthur* in which he brought together the varied strands of the Arthurian legends. The Holy Grail ('Sangrail') remains a drinking vessel, but one that is escorted by angels. On achieving it in company with Sir Percival and Sir Bors, Sir Galahad dies and his companions see his soul borne to heaven by a great multitude of angels. Then a hand descends from heaven: 'And then it came right to the vessel, and took it and the spear, and so bare it up into heaven.' It is interesting to note that the Spear still keeps in company with the Grail almost 1,500 years after they first came together. From that moment on, 'there was never a man so hardy to say that he had seen the Sangrail'.

Over the succeeding centuries, awareness of the Arthurian legends and the Holy Grail gradually died away, until the mid-nineteenth century when interest was revived by the publication of Tennyson's *Idylls of the King*. The theme was taken up by the pre-Raphaelite painters who, in company with Tennyson's work, set off Grail searches in fact and fiction which continue to this day. As if to remark upon this fact, a statue of Tennyson stands in the grounds of Lincoln Cathedral, just a few yards from Bishop Sutton's tomb.

In the meantime, the chalice, standing alongside the bones of Bishop Sutton, had a miraculous escape when Henry VIII's Reformation zealots set about destroying much of the cathedral's shrines and tombs. The shrines of St Hugh were looted and reduced to rubble to such an extent that no one can be sure where the shrine that held the saint's body was situated. The head shrine was severely damaged, but the bulk of it remains today. Other bishops' tombs were destroyed, but Bishop Sutton, having been buried underground, escaped the depredation. Much of what escaped Henry VIII's men fell to the ravages of Cromwellian troopers, who stabled their horses in the cathedral. The tomb (with, by now, the chalice, paten, etc. in the cathedral treasury) also escaped along with the remainder of the cathedral during the Second World War.

In March 1942 the Royal Air Force bombed the unde-fended medieval town of Lubeck, a raid in which the town 'went up in flames'. The Germans launched a series of retali-atory raids against targets with 'three stars in the Baedeker Guide'. These 'Baedeker Raids' attacked the historic cities of Exeter, York, Norwich and Bath. Later, Canterbury was added to the list. The ancient Guildhall at York and the Bath Assembly Rooms were destroyed, along with many other buildings of note. However, the most obvious target for any bomber leaving Germany – Lincoln Cathedral (the highest point in Europe west of the Urals) – escaped due to the fact that the German air force used it as a navigational marker for their raids elsewhere.

There may be some who would claim this as a series of miracles which saved the chalice from loss or destruction over the centuries. They are, of course, entitled so to do. What is not a miracle, but is worthy of note, is that the old tales talk of the Holy Grail being a chalice – and on that simple fact, these chronicles have emerged.

This search for the Holy Grail began with the reading of a biography of Eleanor of Aquitaine. It then went back to the time of the Crucifixion and the appearance of the first Christians in Antioch. From there it saw the Crusades, the rise of the Angevins and Plantagenets, and the formation of the Knights Templar. It saw the influence of the Grail reach and amend the Arthurian legends, and the subsequent rise of a fictional Grail escorted by maidens and angels and bathed in supernatural light. It saw the death of a grasping archbishop and a worthless king, and witnessed the rise of a young knight from obscurity to become the Regent of England. It saw the Grail stand beside the bones of a worthy man for almost 600 years, only to emerge into the light of day unrecognised.

SELECTED BIBLIOGRAPHY

Anon, St. Mary's Mortehoe, Leaflet.

Barlow, Frank, *Thomas Becket*, Guild Publishing, London, 1986.

Billings, Malcolm, *The Crusades, Five Centuries of Holy Wars*, Sterling Publishing Co. Inc., New York, 1996.

Coleman E.C., 'The Book of the Grail'. Unpublished transcription of *The High History of the Holy Grail*, translation by Sebastian Evans, 1898.

Crouch, David, *William Marshal, Knighthood, War and Chivalry, 1147–1219*, Longman, Pearson Education Ltd, Harlow, 2002.

Davis, H.W.C., *Medieval Europe*, Williams & Norgate, London, 1915.

Eyton, R.W. Court, *Household and Itinerary of King Henry II*, London, 1878.

Ferris, Eleanor, *The Financial Relations of the Knights Templar to the English Crown*, The American Historical Review, Vol. 8, No 1, October 1902.

Gillingham, John, *The Life and Times of Richard I*, Weidenfeld & Nicolson, London, 1973.

Guerber, H.A., *Myths of the Norsemen*, George G. Harrap & Co., London, 1919.

Hallam, E. (ed.), *Chronicles of the Age of Chivalry*, Weidenfeld & Nicolson, London, 1987.

————, *The Plantagenet Chronicles*, Tiger Books International, London, 1995.

Harris, Sir Nicholas, *A Chronicle of London from 1089 to 1483*, Longman, Hurst, Rees, Orme, Brown and Green, London, 1827.

Hill, R.M.T. (ed.), *The Rolls and Register of Bishop Oliver Sutton, 1280–1299*, The Lincoln Record Society, 1948.

Kendrick, A.F., *The Cathedral Church of Lincoln*, G. Bell and Sons Ltd, London, 1928.

Lloyd, Alan, *King John*, David & Charles, Newton Abbot, 1973.

Mallory, Sir Thomas, *Sir Thomas Malory's Tales of King Arthur*, Guild Publishing, Book Club Associates, London, 1980.

Matthews, John, *The Grail, The Quest for the Eternal*, Thames and Hudson Ltd, London, 1981.

Meade, Marion, *Eleanor of Aquitaine*, Phoenix Press, London, 2003.

Ralls, Karen, *The Templars and the Grail, Knights of the Quest*, Quest Books, Wheaton, Illinois & Chennai (Madras), India, 2003.

Saunders, J. Junior, *The History of the County of Lincolnshire, from the Earliest Period to the Present Time*, 1833.

de Schalby, John, *The Book of John de Schalby*, translation by J.H.S. Rawley DD, Friends of Lincoln Cathedral, 1948.

Stabb, J., *Some Old Devon Churches*, Simkin, London, 1908.

Stanley, Arthur P., *Historical Memorials of Canterbury*, John Murray, London, 1872.

Vincent, Nicholas, *The Holy Blood, King Henry III and the Westminster Blood Relic*, Cambridge University Press, Cambridge, 2001.

Venables, Rev., *The Archaeological Journal*, Vol. 46, pp. 114–19: The Precentor, 'Opening of the Tomb of Bishop Oliver Sutton, and the Discovery of a Chalice, Paten, and Episcopal Ring', Longmans, Green & Co., London, 1889.

Wallace-Murphy, T., *The Knights of the Holy Grail*, Watkins Publishing, London, 2007.

Waters, Richard, *The Lost Treasure of King John*, Tucann Books, Heighington, Lincoln, 2006.

Weston, J.L., *From Ritual to Romance*, Cambridge University Press, Cambridge, 1920.

INDEX

Alexios I 14
Alfred, Lord Tennyson 157
Alkborough 56, 57
Angel Choir 7, 12, 144, 148
Anson, Admiral Lord
    George 9
Antioch 12–24, 29, 132,
    158
Archbishop Robert
    Kilwardby 133, 135–7
Archbishop Robert
    Winchelsey 146
Archbishop Walter Gifford
    140
Aymeric de St Maur 101

Baldur 67, 69
Battle of Arsuf 91, 92
Battle of Camlann 70, 153
Battle of Dorylaon 15
Battle of La Forbie 131
Benedictines 40

Berengaria of Navarre 87,
    88, 101
Bernard of Clairvaux 21,
    39–43, 107, 140
Bishop Adhemar de
    Monteil 16
Bishop Hugh of Lincoln 80,
    97, 98, 141–4, 153, 157
Bishop Oliver Sutton 140,
    141, 144–54, 157, 158
Bishop Pandalf 120, 121, 124
Bishop Remigious 147
Bohemund II 18
Bohemund of Taranto 14–6
Byzantine Empire 14, 15

Chapel of the Grail 77, 79
Chrétien de Troyes 65, 70, 72
Conrad III 19, 22
Constantinople 14, 16, 86,
    129, 138
Council of Clarendon 33, 46

Count Phillip of Flanders 65,
    80, 86
Crown of Thorns 8, 11, 35,
    49, 126–8, 138

Dominican Order 132, 133,
    136, 137, 155
Duke Leopold of Austria 87,
    88, 94

Earl of Salisbury 64, 72, 81, 112
Edessa 19–22, 144
Edward Grim 55
Eleanor of Castile 130, 133,
    134, 144
Eleanor of Provence 125
Emperor Constantine 14, 156
Emperor Frederick I 86, 87
Emperor Isaac Angleus 86, 87
Emperor Isaac Comnenus 86

Falkes de Breaute 117, 121,
    122
Fatimid Arabs 13–5
Fisher King 75
Foxes' Book of Martyrs 106,
    107
Frig 67, 69

Gerald de Ridefort 81, 87, 90
Glastonbury 71
Godfrey of Bouillon 14, 17, 38
Great Schism 14
Guy de Lusignan 64, 72, 81, 90

Holy Blood 127–9
Holy Grail 8, 9, 70–9, 119,
    139, 140, 145, 148, 151–9
Holy Sepulchre 14, 16, 22,
    39, 74, 82, 114, 132
Horns of Hattin 82, 87, 92
Hubert de Burgh 107, 119–24
Huge de Morville 52–6, 96
Hugh of Horsea 55
Hughes de Payens 38–42, 45

Isabel de Clare 114
Isabelle of Angouleme 98
Isabelle of Gloucester 98
Islam 12, 13, 61, 62, 91, 92, 101
Italian Merchant Bankers
    125, 135, 139

Jerusalem 14–9, 22, 24, 38, 39,
    45, 55, 58, 72, 79, 81, 82,
    87–94, 114, 127, 129, 132,
    134, 154
Jews 100, 124, 126, 135, 143
John FitzGilbert 34, 64
Joseph of Arimathea 72–5,
    105, 137

Khwarezmian Tartars 127
King Alexander of Scotland
    103, 104
King Alphonso X of Castile
    130
King Arthur 65–74, 77–9, 96,
    104, 119, 153, 157, 159

King Edward I 134–9, 145, 146, 153, 157
King Edward the Confessor 52, 121, 126
King Henry II 26–37, 46, 50, 51, 55, 56, 63, 65, 80, 81, 84–7, 97, 105, 113, 114
King Henry III 86, 115, 121–31, 135, 139, 140
King John 37, 63, 81, 84, 87, 88, 93–119, 143
King Louis VI 21
King Louis VII 19–29, 47, 63, 65, 80
King Phillip II 84–8, 93, 95, 99–103, 115
King Richard I 58, 63, 65, 80–97, 101, 114, 120, 143
King Stephen 25–7, 30, 45
King Tancred of Sicily 17, 87, 94
King William I of Scotland 85
Knights Hospitaller 81, 91, 92
Knights Templar 40–9, 57, 61, 81, 82, 85–94, 100–5, 122–41, 145, 155–7

Lance of Longinus 8–17, 23, 35, 44, 70–7, 84, 138
Last Supper 9, 49, 72, 105, 128, 137, 154
Lincoln 25, 31, 34, 100, 103, 104, 107, 116, 117, 121, 140, 141, 153

Lincoln Imp 148–52
Loki 69, 70
Longinus 9, 70, 129

Marguerite of France 113
Marie of Champagne 21, 26, 65
Martel, Charles 13
Mortehoe 58, 59

Nail (relic) 8, 35, 62
Nettleham 148, 150
Nettleham Church 150
Newark 106, 116, 117
Nicaea 14
Nicola de la Haye 103, 116, 117

Patriarch of Jerusalem 127–9
Perlesvaux 73, 79
Peter Bartholomew 15
Peter de Rivaux 120, 124
Peter des Roches 120–5, 133
Peter the Hermit 14
Pope Eugenius III 19, 21, 43
Pope Gregory VIII 82
Pope Gregory IX 123, 124
Pope Honorius III 105, 144
Pope Nicholas III 138
Pope Urban II 14
Pope Urban III 82
Prince Arthur 98, 99, 103, 114, 119
Prince Geoffrey 63, 80, 81, 98

Prince Henry (Young King Henry) 49, 50, 53, 63–5, 80, 113, 114
Prince Llewelyn 122, 123
Prince Louis of France 102, 103, 111, 119
Prince Raymond of Antioch 18–25, 29
Prince Robert de Artois 132
Prince William 31, 33, 35, 46

Queen Eleanor of Aquitaine 19–29, 36, 37, 47, 49, 63–5, 72, 80–7, 95–8, 112, 114, 119, 136, 144, 154, 158
Queen Guinevere 69
Queen Matilda 25–6, 45, 104

Ragnarok 69, 71
Ranulf de Broc 34, 50–3
Raymond IV 14
Reginald FitzUrse 51–5
Richard de Humet 51
Richard le Bret 52, 55
Robert Burnell 136, 137
Robert de Boron 72
Robert de Gresley 111
Robert de Sable 90
Robert de Waleran 136
Robert Twenge (William Wither) 124
Rosamund de Clifford 37, 80

Saher de Quincy 51
Sainte Chapelle 126, 128, 139, 155
Saladin 81–95
Seljuk Turks 13
Simon de Montfort 130, 131, 140
Sir Bedivere 68
Sir Gawain 68, 70, 74–9
Sir Lancelot 70, 79, 90, 96
Sir Mordred 69, 70
Sir Percival 65, 70, 74, 75, 77–9
Sir Thomas Malory 72, 157
St Helen 14
Statute of Mortmain 138, 139
Stow 116
Swineshead Abbey 106, 110, 111, 119

Temple of Solomon 16, 37, 39, 40
The Wash 104, 105
Thomas Becket 28–37, 46, 49–64, 71, 85, 96, 112, 119, 127
Thor 67–71
Torksey 116
True Cross 8, 24, 35, 49, 82, 88, 93, 126, 128, 138
Tyr 67–9

Walter of Hemingford 106
William Caxton 106
William Chillenden 136

William de Braose 123

William de Manderville (Earl of Essex) 51

William de Tancarville 112, 113

William de Tracy 52–60

William Longchamp 88

William Marshal 45, 64, 96, 105, 106, 112–20, 130

William Shakespeare 106, 107

Woden 66–9